WAKING
TO
GOD'S
DREAM

WAKING TO GOD'S DREAM

Spiritual Leadership
and Church Renewal

DICK WILLS

ABINGDON PRESS
NASHVILLE

WAKING TO GOD'S DREAM
SPIRITUAL LEADERSHIP AND CHURCH RENEWAL

Copyright © 1999 by Abingdon Press

This book is printed on recycled, acid-free paper.

Library of Congress Cataloging-in-Publication Data

Wills, Dick, 1942—
    Waking to God's dream: spiritual leadership and church renewal/
Dick Wills.
        p. cm.
    ISBN 0-687-00482-9 (alk. paper)
    1. Church renewal—United Methodist Church (U.S.) 2. Christian leadership—United Methodist Church (U.S.) 3. Spiritual life— United Methodist Church (U.S.) I. Title.
    BX8382.2.W57   1999
    262'.001'7—dc21
                                                            99-10345
                                                                 CIP

01 02 03 04 05 06 07 08 — 10 9 8 7 6 5

MANUFACTURED IN THE UNITED STATES OF AMERICA

To my loving wife, Eileen

ACKNOWLEDGMENTS

My deepest gratitude goes to a gracious and patient God, revealed in Jesus Christ, who continues to love me and shape me in spite of my pride and arrogance over many years of Christian ministry. God just refused to give up on me, and I am most thankful.

I would like to acknowledge the enormous help given to me in creating this book. I wish to thank Neil Alexander and Ezra Earl Jones for their continued invitations to record what God is doing in my life and in the life of Christ Church.

I am grateful to many pastors who have encouraged me with this book: Phil Roughton, Jim Harnish, Jorge Acevedo, Tom Hamilton, Tony Chance, and Ken Brown are among so many pastors who have given encouragement. Debbie Mcleod not only encouraged me, but also read and reread the material so that it could be presented in a readable form. Her support as one of the pastors at Christ Church has in many ways made this book possible.

I want the readers to know that without the loving support of my wife, Eileen, this book would never have been written. She took time off from her work to help me with the manuscript. She has been and is the love of my life for which I will forever be grateful.

Finally, I would like to acknowledge the people of Christ Church who were willing to be led in a new way that is both biblical and spiritual. I am deeply grateful for the 122 Lay Pastors who lead the ministries of Christ Church. They have taught me much about living as a servant of God.

Christ Church sponsors a Visitation Weekend on the second weekend of each month. This is a teaching-learning opportunity that Christ Church offers to clergy, staff, and laity who would like to know more about Christ Church and the principles that guide the church. Please write or call Christ Church for more information:

dwills@christchurchum.org

Christ Church
4845 NE 25 Avenue
Fort Lauderdale, Florida 33308
954-771-7300

CONTENTS

FOREWORD

by James Harnish

This book may challenge, threaten, disturb, or inspire you. Two questions about Dick Wills and the story he tells define the reason this book may turn you off and the reason you need to read it. The first question: Is this guy for real?

The directness, candor, and clarity with which Dick talks about his spiritual life and leadership can be downright uncomfortable for many of us who have been conditioned to speak cautiously of these things. One person got it right when he told me, "Dick doesn't hedge his bets in the God business the way most of us do." Dick tells—and lives!—the story of what God has done in his life without arrogance, but with a deep sense of what the Methodist tradition calls "assurance." He is absolutely sure that God does in fact speak, move, and act in his experience. He is confident that the principles he has learned are the tools through which God has transformed his life and is leading him in ministry. Unfortunately, we are often conditioned to respond with a mixture of cynicism and distrust to the disarmingly direct way in which a person like Dick talks of God. It makes some folks wonder if the guy has a hidden agenda. Others will wonder if the guy who tells the story is for real.

I've known Dick for more than twenty-five years. As colleagues in the ministry, we've laughed, cried, worked, traveled, played, and worshiped together at the Warren Willis Youth Camp (named in memory of the father-in-law Dick describes in this book), in the local churches to which we have been appointed, in denominational conferences and programs, in movie theaters, and over countless cups of coffee. I have had the privilege of being an eye witness to the transformation he describes in this book. Step by step, I have observed the struggle and surrender, the joy and pain, the discouragement and discovery through which God has been at work in his life and, through his leadership, in the life of Christ Church, Fort Lauderdale.

At times I've questioned Dick's assumptions, probed his feelings, and pushed him toward the next phase of his journey. But most of the time I have watched in hungering amazement as God has hallowed, carved, and shaped Dick's heart. I've followed his movement from being an effective institutional church pastor into living a life of spiritual leadership that is centered in a consistent life of prayer. I've seen the effect this transformation has had on the people around him, some of it positive and some of it filled with pain. Through it all, I have been challenged by the intentionality of his obedience and the integrity of his faith. There is nothing phony or artificial about this man's life with God. When he talks about obedience to Jesus, he obeys. When he talks about prayer, he prays. This guy is absolutely authentic. This story is for real.

The second defining question is: What's in this for me?

Dick's story can be downright threatening because it forces us to ask: Why don't we talk like that? Why are we hesitant to speak with humble assurance about God's will? Why are we afraid to be as simple, clear, and direct about our desire to introduce people to Jesus? And perhaps the most important question: What might it mean for me to live and lead out of that kind of obedience, centered in a life of prayer?

It's no exaggeration for me to say that Dick's spiritual journey has marked the path that many of us are following. I am among a surprising number of pastors who have seen in Dick's ministry something of God's new calling for our own. By observing what the Spirit of God is doing at Christ Church, we have caught a glimpse of God's vision for the church we lead. In the honesty of his costly obedience to the love of God, we have found courage to take more costly risks in our leadership as well. Being touched by his life of prayer, we have been held more accountable for our own spiritual discipline.

I once heard Dr. Donald English, for many years the spiritual voice of British Methodism, say that the world doesn't need any more salespersons for the gospel, but the world desperately needs more free samples. For many of us, Dick has become a "free sample" of God's vision for spiritual leadership in our time. Christ Church has become a living model of a church that intentionally focuses its energies on sharing the love of God in Jesus with the secular, searching, suffering culture around us. It's not as if Dick ever intended to be a model to the rest of us. Far from it. He was simply attempting—sometimes out of desperation!—to be faithful to the call that God placed on his life in the context of the congregation he was appointed to serve. But God has used him to lure, tug, or push some of us into a deeper life of prayer, a clearer sense of calling, and a more energetic level of spiritual leadership.

I encourage you to read this book with an open mind and a receptive heart. It may be that God will use it in your life as well.

INTRODUCTION

Some time ago I was invited to go on a Sunday evening to hear John Nesbitt speak on the New World Order. Nesbitt, author of *Megatrends* and *Megatrends 2000* said that evening that we are experiencing a time of *shift in orientation*. Years ago, our time orientation was to the past. When it was time to plant the crops, you went to your dad or granddad and asked how and when to plant. In the Industrial Age, the orientation was to the present. The question was, "How can we make it better *now*?" Today, time orientation is to the future. What do we want the future to look like in the year 2000 and beyond? By looking to the future, we can determine what happens today. Nesbitt said, "As we look to the year 2000 and beyond, it is only a short time away." Nesbitt was saying that it is important for us to vision the future.

As I listened to him, I thought to myself, "That's nothing new." God has always been futuring for God's people. When God spoke to Moses, he didn't tell him how it was in the past. God didn't vision in the present to tell how life could be more bearable in slavery. No, God told Moses to lead God's people out of Egypt and into their future in the promised land. Jesus talked about the Kingdom that was coming in the future but that is also here now. God has always been calling God's people into the future.

I want to give you an important principle for any church, any person, or any home:

"It is not what you are now that is important, but what God wants you to be and what you can be with faith."

"Where there is no prophecy, the people cast off restraint" (Proverbs 29:18 NRSV). The King James Version says, "Where there is no vision, the people perish." The Hebrew term for vision is *chazon*; it usually means "revelation" or "what God wants you to be."

A vision is what God wants you to do and be. But there is more. If a vision is to be more than an empty dream, it needs a *task*.

When hurricane Andrew struck South Florida, we in Fort Lauderdale were fortunate to have been spared most of the damage. Immediately there was a call for food and water to aid families farther south whose homes had been destroyed. Through the Wesley Fellowship Groups (small group ministry) in our church, we were able, within a few hours time, to fill most of our fellowship hall with much needed food and water. Most of the people in small groups brought food and water in just a few hours. That afternoon, a man called me and said he had been watching television and saw that we were one of the food distribution points. The man wondered, "What can one man do?" He called a moving van company and that company was willing to bring their largest moving van, an 18-wheeler, to the church and transport the food and water south to Dade County. When that giant moving van pulled up to our fellowship hall, I walked in and saw one or two volunteers in a room that was filled almost to the ceiling with bottled water and boxes of food. Earlier that afternoon most of the volunteers had left. I said to the one person who was still present, "How are we ever going to fill this moving van so that we can take it to South Dade County?" The woman simply winked at me, picked up a box, and said, "Dick, we are going to do this one box at a time."

We had a *vision* to take food to the people in South Dade County, and we had a task to move the boxes from the fellowship hall into the moving van. It was the task that made the *vision* become a reality. But, I can tell you that just picking up boxes one at a time can be pure drudgery. It's not good enough just to have a task. A task needs to have a vision—a vision that is not where you are now, but where God wants you to be. A vision is what makes the task exciting and alive with purpose. Without a vision, a task is just drudgery.

A vision without a task is just a dream. We have all known people who have read a book or gone to a seminar and then come back with a vision, but no way to make that vision a reality. The vision has no task and it simply becomes a dream that fizzles out. I suspect that if we are honest we would have to admit that has happened to almost all of us.

A task without a vision is pure drudgery. Without a vision the tasks of church life deteriorate into endless dreary committee meetings. A church that has a vision with no task is just a church that dreams while it decays.

What can happen to a church, an individual, a business, or a home when a vision and a task come together? It can become the hope of the world.

That happened to John Wesley. When someone asked him what could be reasonably expected of a Methodist preacher, he replied, "To reform the Nation and the Church and to spread scriptural holiness over the land." When you combine a vision and a task it can become the hope of the world.

A vision is seeing not what is now, but what can be and will be in the future. Too many people see only what is now, or only what has been. Someone told me that God put eyes in the front so that when we look backward, we get a stiff neck. God wants us to look forward. God gives every person, every family, every church a vision to see what it can be and what it will be in the future.

Whenever a vision involves a group, God selects one person to announce that vision on behalf of all the other people. The biblical principle is this:

God gives one person the vision

God plants the vision secretly in the hearts of people. They cannot see the vision until the person God has chosen reveals it. Once the vision is announced, it must be confirmed by the people for whom the vision is given.

Not all visions for the church come through a clergyperson. In 1978 I was appointed to a church at Englewood, Florida, that was already building a mammoth new facility on seventeen acres outside the small community of Englewood. When I did some exploring, I found that a small group of men had met for breakfast every Monday morning for a number of years. Within that group the vision was first shared. God had given a vision for the Englewood Church to one of the laity, a banker in the community. The vision was that the Englewood Church was to buy seventeen acres outside of town and relocate the church!

Excitedly, the men went to the pastor and asked the pastor about purchasing the seventeen acres outside of town. The pastor at the time said, "No, I don't think we'll ever need that kind of land. I don't think that will be possible." That summer the pastor went on vacation. Now, when a vision is inspired by the Holy Spirit, it has a strength of its own. This group of laypeople went to the head of the regional judicatory body and got him to hold an official meeting while the pastor was on vacation. The church voted to buy the seventeen acres of land and voted to relocate the church. When the pastor came back he said, "Well, I guess it's okay." And he went along with it. Today, the Englewood Church is one of the strongest congregations in the state of Florida. It is a church that is vision driven and empowered by the Holy Spirit.

The Bible is full of visionaries. Joshua, Caleb, and ten others were sent to spy on the promised land. Ten people saw what was. They saw difficulties, walls, giants, impossibilities. Joshua and Caleb saw what could be and would be with faith in God. When they got back, Joshua presented a plan for how to enter a land that was, in spite of its difficulties, the land God had promised God's people, one that would flow with milk and honey.

A vision can happen at any point in life. A vision can touch a company, a family, or an individual. A teacher can look at her classroom and can envision what those children can be and will be. A winning football team always has a coach who has been able to envision what the team can be and will be. It happens to a church when people believe the biblical promise that God is able to do new things in spite of current obstacles.

Do you have a vision? Do you know personally what God wants you to be? Do you know what God wants you to be as a husband or as a wife, as a father, as a mother, as a Christian, as a pastor? Do you know what God wants for your church? A recent survey told that 80 to 85 percent of the churches in America are plateaued or dying. This is because they lack a vision of what can be and will be with faith in God.

It could be that a lot of people are conditioned to see the way things are now and only remember how things used to be. Remember Proverbs 29:18, which tells us that without any revelation, without any vision, people go away without purpose. Do you know what God's vision is for you?

How does a vision happen? O. S. Hawkins, the former senior pastor of First Baptist Church in Dallas, Texas, shared with me that he believes a vision happens much like childbirth.

First, there is *conception*. The seed of a man and woman come together and there is life. God gives the seed of a vision to a particular individual. It is a seed of what can be and what will be.

The next stage is *gestation*. There is something happening. The vision is growing. Although no one can see the vision, it is quietly developing in the person to whom God has given the vision. In the Old Testament, God gave Joseph a vision of leadership, a vision that stayed within him for many years, even through the years he was in prison. God's vision for Christ Church, where I am pastor, grew within me for more than two years before I knew it and was ready to share it.

And then, after a time of gestation, something happens. Birth! Nobody who gives birth to a child is able to keep quiet. We always want to share with others: "It's a girl!" "It's a boy!" When a vision is born, we are not able to keep quiet. It is announced. The vision must be announced long enough for one to know that the vision is from God and not just another voice in one's head. (In my case I announced the vision for a year before I knew that it was a vision from God to our church.) God plants the vision secretly in the hearts of God's people, even though they might not be aware of it. However, when it is announced, it wins acceptance from those committed to God because God had made it their vision, secretly, sometime before.

The next stage is *claiming*. New parents eagerly claim their new infant as their very own. A lot of visions end up at zero because people never claim it for their own. In each local church whatever God's vision is for the people, it must be claimed by a majority of people. This is a scary time. The risk is that you may have been listening not to the voice of God but to other voices. If this is God's vision for you, then God will also have planted it secretly in the hearts of most of the people.

The next stage is *growth*, or *childhood*. When a vision is accepted by people and claimed as their own, a tremendous amount of energy is released. It can be a dangerous time because it creates so many changes. Ask anyone who has ever raised children. It costs money and creates turmoil; it is a time of growth that carries great potential to produce hurt. With children, we understand that the potential for hurt is simply the cost we pay for the growth that takes place. In the church, we understand that the growth that comes through the empowerment of the Holy Spirit can also hurt because it is such a time of change.

The next stage is *maturity*. This is where the vision comes to fruition. Throughout its history Methodism's vision has matured and then reproduced. If you are familiar with The United Methodist Church, would you say this denomination matured in the 1950s and 1960s? If that is true, then we should be seeing a denomination that is in a time of a great new vision. The United Methodist Church has been in a consistent decline since the late 1960s. Could it be that God is looking for men and women who will speak a new vision for this denomination? What has brought us this far will not be adequate to take us to the new vision that God has for this denomination. I believe this is true of most mainline denominations.

Now there is one more step, perhaps the most important. It is *reproduction*. A vision either dies or is reproduced into a new vision. God is always ready to give a new vision when the old vision comes to maturity. Otherwise, the vision simply dies and perishes. Mainline denominations are declining because leaders have not been willing to listen to the God who is seeking to reproduce the vision for a new day. It is very easy to be a person who trusts God in a daily walk, but then become the very kind of person who is unwilling to walk in new and different directions. When this change takes place, it is always the sign that the vision is dying.

Almost four hundred years ago the Pilgrims came across the Atlantic Ocean in a voyage that took vision and courage. They sailed uncharted seas and traveled thousands of miles to follow their vision. In the first year that they were here, they established a town. In the second year they established a town council. In the third year the town council voted to build a road five miles into the wilderness. In the fourth year they almost impeached the town council for trying to build a road five miles into the wilderness. They said it was a terrible waste of money. A people once empowered by a vision to travel across the ocean were now a people who could not see five miles into the wilderness. A vision has to be reproduced.

The church I serve had grown rapidly some years ago because of a vision that God gave to a pastor of the church. Christ Church reached a point where the vision had grown and matured. Then the church began to slip backward. In January of 1992 new spiritual vitality came to Christ Church through the small group ministries that had begun. I could tell that there was much spiritual power in our church, but I was clueless about what it was that God wanted our church to become. I knew I had to spend some time with God to try to understand what it was that God wanted for Christ Church. I wanted to be part of what God was blessing!

In September 1992, I went away for a week to pray and fast. During that week God's vision for Christ Church became clear to me. It was not very complex. It is, in fact, very simple. God's vision for our church was to do just three things:

1. To introduce people to Jesus in positive ways
2. To disciple believers through Wesley Fellowship Groups (small group ministry)
3. To relieve suffering

Remember Proverbs 29:18 (KJV): "Where there is no vision, the people perish." Where there is no vision, there is no purpose.

On Easter morning the empty tomb brought no one to faith. But Mary talked to Jesus and came to faith when she heard Jesus call her name. The voice of Jesus calling her by name opened her to the power of God to work wonders. Like the voice that shatters glass, the voice of Jesus shattered Mary's world and called her forward to new possibilities and a new future.

Mary was now able to obey and to tell others, "I have seen the Lord" (John 20:18 NIV). She recognized his face. And the rest is the history of her vision and faith. Have you heard Jesus call your name?

This book is about listening to the voice of God and discovering where you are going. It's not where you have come from, but where you are going that is important. Where is your church going? Do you know God's vision for you, for your family, for your church? God has a vision and a plan for you just as God does for me. I don't know the vision that God has for you or your church. I do know that what is needed in our time is pastors and laity who are willing to be part of what God is blessing. Here are some of the ingredients you can be sure will be part of God's vision for you and your church.

1. It will deal with Kingdom issues. It will be a vision that you will also see in the Bible. The Bible is the key to understanding what kind of things God gives us to do.
2. It will be larger than you or your church can do by your own energy. It will be so big that you will have to depend on God to make it happen.
3. It will be clear. A lot of Christian groups are good at making clear directives fuzzy. It will not be fuzzy.
4. It will usually take a group of people to carry out the vision.

FOR REFLECTION

1. At what stage is the vision God has given to you or your church?
2. Have the ministries of your church become a drudgery?
3. Do you sense God doing a new thing?
4. How are you doing spending time with God daily so that you can be part of what God wants to bless?

CHAPTER ONE

Telling the Story

Success Track

I was the firstborn child of my family; my two sisters were born later. As the firstborn I was taught to do the right thing. Firstborn children often grow up a little faster than other children do. I think that happened to me. I was the child who wanted to succeed at whatever I attempted, as well as to please people and to be loved.

Working hard was the norm of my earliest memories. When I was old enough to play Little League baseball, my dad signed me up and even volunteered to be an assistant coach. He worked with me to help me learn the game. I can remember my first summer in Little League. I went to every practice, but I never played in a game that first summer. Only the best players were allowed to play. I had contracted polio when I was one year old. One of my legs is smaller than the other, but I never felt at a disadvantage to the other players. Even though I did not play, I worked very hard; and in my last year of Little League baseball, I had the highest batting average in the league. Hard work had paid off, though I was surprised that I had done so well. A good work ethic would later be a contributing factor in the way I would answer God's call into the ministry.

I first felt the call to ministry when I was in the seventh grade. I was walking on a dirt road in Texas on my way to nowhere on a hot summer day. I was just a few blocks from my home. I was thinking about life, and it just seemed that Jesus wanted me to be a minister. Shortly after that experience my parents told me my dad had been transferred to Florida. After moving to Miami, Florida, I became active in a local church. The church was evangelical, and its message about Jesus confirmed the call I felt from Jesus on that dusty road in South Houston, Texas. I was going to be a minister.

Of all my family, my grandmother Bessie Hanna was the one who offered me the most encouragement. In fact, until her death in 1982 she would call me regularly to talk about the things of God. It was not uncommon for her to phone me at five o'clock on a Sunday morning before I was to preach. She would ask me a question like: "Dickie, do you know how many times love is mentioned in 1 John?" I would answer, "No, Granny, I have no idea how many times love is mentioned in First John." She would then tell me the answer, "Thirty-three times," and close by saying, "Don't forget today that love is the most important force in the world! Good-bye!" and hang up. Denominations never seemed to matter to her. Just because I was in one denomination and she was in another never became a point of conversation. Jesus was all that mattered. She was delighted to hear of my call to ministry.

After high school, I worked summers at our denominational youth camp. It was at the youth camp that I met Eileen, the most special person in my life. Five years later she would become my wife. Her dad, Warren Willis, was a minister and the director of the summer camping programs in our state. He would become my mentor in a very special way.

I graduated from a Christian college and enrolled immediately in seminary. My seminary days were filled with study, getting married, and working as a youth pastor in a church near the seminary. All of these events confirmed my sense of God's calling me into ministry.

At some point during my seminary years, I experienced a shift in focus. The word *career* quietly replaced *calling* in my life. My denomination never taught that my life was about becoming a success in a *career*, but firstborn child that I was, I quickly learned what it would take to be a success. It was all about *career*. I was not just a follower of Jesus; now I was also someone who had to make his way in the world. I would be in charge of my career; God would be a very distant second in my life. God had given me all the things I needed to work out life my own way. Secretly, I wanted to be well thought of by people, especially my peers. I would simply follow the external rules of my denomination to make my way to the top of the career ladder.

I understood that to be successful in a ministry career, I must do the things my denomination told me to do and do them as well as I could. I expected, initially, to be assigned to a little church with a handful of sheep. If I did well with them, then I would be assigned to another church that would be larger, pay more in salary, and have more sheep. I understood I would keep doing that until one day my denomination would recognize me for being successful and give me an assignment that did not have any sheep. I know this sounds strange, but that is the way I understood my denominational system to work.

I did all the things my denomination told me to do. As promised, my denomination kept rewarding me with larger churches and more sheep. I was on the "success track" in my *career*. I had been chosen by my peers to chair a judicatory board that reviews and recommends candidates for ordained ministry. Almost everyone who knew me would have said that I was definitely a success in my denomination. However, all of that would change when I was assigned to Christ Church in 1986.

Christ Church was a large-membership church that had suffered through a very painful time. I was the third senior pastor in four years. I believe the person who headed the music department was largely responsible for holding the church together during this time of rapid rotation of senior ministers. The church focused with some pride on its classical music program. Just about a year before I was assigned, the music director became ill with a terrible disease. Eventually, he was released from service at Christ Church. His departure in January of 1986 divided the congregation. I arrived at Christ Church five months later.

The church was in a difficult place financially and was being held together by the remaining wonderful staff and a core of very dedicated laity. I began doing all the things my denomination had taught me to do in order to be successful in my career. The harder I worked, the better things seemed to go at the church. Being a firstborn child who wants to do the right thing, I gave Christ Church my all. I even gave the church time I should have been spending with my family. But then, I wanted to be a success in my *career,* and any sacrifice would be worth it. Or would it?

BONE-WEARINESS

By 1991 I had become weary of doing good. I still wanted to please people, and deep down I wanted to be loved. When I had a lot of energy, the church seemed to do well. But as my energy ran low, the church seemed not to do as well. This was a time when I felt that everything depended on me. My energy level had to remain high just to keep the church from slipping backward. I went to so many meetings that really did not seem to matter. I felt the strength within me ebbing away. I did all the right things. I preached each week and was faithful to the biblical text. I made hospital visits weekly, kept regular office hours, visited, supported other groups in the church, counseled troubled individuals, had numerous breakfast and lunch appointments, prayed whenever asked, and spent very little time with my family. This was what I understood to be the path to success.

I went to hundreds of meetings at Christ Church in those first five years. As I look back now, most of those meetings really did not do anything for the Kingdom. All they did was to take up a huge amount of my time. My involvement in all those committee meetings really did little more than keep the organization alive. In fact, I had led our people in such a way that we had substituted meetings for ministry. By focusing on my career and wanting to please people, I had left behind the things of God and the power of the Holy Spirit.

I was very tired and weary. I was tired because of the emotional strain I had been under for such a long time trying to get this church to do better. I was weary because without the power of the Holy Spirit, the work I was doing was all on my own. I began to think that if I could be the pastor of another church, then my life would not be so wearisome. Perhaps my denomination would send me to another (better) church. Or since I was too young to retire, maybe I would be able to keep my career path on line and not have to serve a local church. I began to know why some middle-aged males begin to hope to be called to do something on the denominational level. You can get so weary that you will do anything, as long as it is different. The weariness from trying to do good, be loved, and to have a successful career was really a spiritual issue. My weariness came from having left behind a daily walk with God, substituting in its place taking control and wanting to be successful in the eyes of others.

In 1990 a good friend of mine told me he had really enjoyed his time spent attending a World Methodist Evangelism event. I thought that an event far from home might provide the relief I needed from my weariness. I sent for a brochure that said the World Methodist Evangelism

Conference was in Tahiti. I thought to myself, "What a wonderful place to do evangelism—Tahiti!" I applied and a few weeks later received word that I was one of about ten North Americans accepted to the 1991 event. The only problem was that I had misread the brochure when I applied. The 1991 event was in South Africa! Tahiti was to be the following year.

I felt a sinking sense of disappointment about going to a country that was going through such difficult times. Apartheid was still in effect, and there was much violence and poverty. Yet, I had a compelling feeling that I was supposed to go to South Africa.

The cost of the trip became a problem. Once in South Africa, I needed to pay only $200 for the ten days of the conference. But the airfare was $2,050! I did not have enough continuing education funds to pay for the airfare, and the church was in no position to grant it to me.

I decided to speak to a wealthy, evangelical layman about my trip. I thought he would say, "Dick, that's great! Let me pay for the airfare!" But when I presented him with the opportunity, he said, "Dick I don't think you should go. I think you need to stay here and help us raise the money for our new Life Enrichment Center." I did not know what to do. I felt I was supposed to go, but there were no funds for the airfare. I did not pray about this, because at this time in my life I only prayed in public settings and when asked. I did not have a daily walk with God. I was still trying to be in control.

The trip was one month away, and I still did not have the funds for the airfare. A stranger came to our early service one Sunday. As he went out the door, he said, "I was praying this morning, and I am supposed to give this to you." It was an envelope. I slipped the envelope into my hymnal. After the services that day I opened the envelope. It was a check made out to me for $2,000! I knew I was supposed to use it for my airfare to South Africa.

I left for South Africa in May of 1991. The day I arrived

there had been bombings in Johannesburg where the World Methodist Evangelism Conference was to be held. I can remember telling the man who picked me up from the airport that I was uneasy being there. *Scared* is a better word. He said to me, "Dick, you don't have to be afraid anymore because now you are surrounded by the loving arms of the church." And he was right. I was never afraid from that point on.

There were two hundred people at the event. They came from all over central and southern Africa. Most were very poor and enduring great hardships. I was immediately struck by their obvious joy. I began to wonder how these people, living under such difficult and violent conditions could have such joy? It was a stark contrast to my own situation. I live in one of the most affluent areas of Fort Lauderdale, Florida. I have a wonderful family and a beautiful home. I am serving one of the most prominent churches in my denomination. I had every mark of success. Why was it these people in Africa had this joy and I did not? I knew I wanted that joy in my own life.

Halfway through the conference I was told that there would be a "hymn sing" on Saturday evening. I am not much on singing, and after about twenty minutes I am usually ready to move on to another activity. On that Saturday evening, I deliberately took a seat on the back row. I thought I would be there for about twenty minutes and then slip out to go back to my room and do some reading. The hymn sing began at seven o'clock. The people began singing; and when I looked at my watch, I discovered it was after ten o'clock. I had been there for three hours! I simply could not believe these people had such a joy and song in their souls. I wanted to know that kind of joy.

I spent time with a number of these people who were very poor. After a while I began to discover that joy was a product of walking with God no matter what your external circumstances. That led me to understand the first principle God was trying to teach me.

Principle 1

Joy comes from walking with God and is not dependent on external circumstances.

NEW LIFE

I cannot point to a specific moment during my trip to South Africa when I experienced rebirth, but rebirth is what happened. I just know I experienced a joy that, since my time in South Africa, has never dissipated. It would be another eight or nine months before I could begin to make sense of what had happened to me there. At the time I knew only that my heart felt different.

My first Sunday back in Fort Lauderdale, I asked the congregation for forgiveness for my lack of spiritual leadership. The strange thing was that no one made any comment to me about that remark. I had hoped that someone would ask me a question about my lack of spiritual leadership. Even though no one questioned me, I think people knew that something important had happened to me in South Africa, but they were not exactly sure what.

My experience in South Africa left me with an openness to begin the journey of choosing to be part of what God wanted to bless rather than my trying to get God to bless what I was doing. Most of my ministry I had been trying to persuade God to bless my good ideas. In a way I was trying to be God. Now I was beginning to see that what God wanted was for me to simply join God in what God was choosing to bless. My new prayer of asking God to help me be part of what God was choosing to bless was important in helping me understand that I am not God and that I am not in control. This has become fundamental in helping me to move from trying to be in control of everything to learning to trust God.

I began to realize what Jesus was talking about in John

3:3: "Jesus said, 'You're absolutely right. Take it from me: Unless a person is born from above, it's not possible to see what I'm pointing to—to God's kingdom' " *(The Message)*.

Since I was now sure that joy was found in learning to be obedient to God, I wanted to learn to trust God with all of my life. So I began to pray each day for God to help me and Christ Church be part of what God wanted to bless.

Principle 2

God blesses obedience.

I am convinced that God blesses obedience. The more I align my life with God's will and learn to give up trying to control and direct so much of life, the better I seem to get along in all areas of my life.

I learned the futility of trying to be in control from my children and from my English bird dog, Alice. I did my best to control our four children. As each child reached adolescence, I gave up trying to tightly control their lives. I retreated to our dog, Alice. If I could not control anyone else, I could control Alice. If I told her to "sit," she would sit. If I told her to "go to her bed," she went to her bed. People were always impressed that I had such control over Alice. Then one day I discovered that Alice obeyed me as long as I had eye contact with her. But when I turned and entered into conversation with another person, Alice would simply do what she had wanted to do all along. She was obedient until I turned my head. I really did not control her at all! Alice taught me that I do not control anyone really—a hard lesson for someone who so wanted to be in control of other people and things as I did.

As I came to realize that I am not really in control of anything—even my dog—it became clear to me that my journey was leading me to choose to give all that controlling stuff to God. I was at the very beginning of choosing to begin to be obedient to God. All of my carefully laid plans must now be put aside, and I would have to begin to trust God with all of my life. This was not an easy choice for a person so used to trying to be in control of life, family, and church. Yet I knew that God would bless me as I began to choose to surrender my life for a brand new life that I had begun to experience in South Africa.

FOR REFLECTION

I suspect that as you read this chapter, you might be thinking about your own call to ministry. Is that call still fresh and the driving motivation of your ministry?

1. Or have you noticed how well you are doing by comparing yourself to your peers?

2. Is the driving motivation of your ministry to climb to the top of the ministry ladder?

3. Do you find yourself looking with some envy at other churches that are doing better than the one you serve?

4. Are you looking to be sent or called to another church?

The way you answer those questions will reveal whether you see your ministry as a call or career. Call gives life. Career sucks the life out of you.

5. What about your church? Do you spend the majority of time in meetings or ministry?

6. Have the people of your church substituted meetings for ministry?

7. What would it be like to serve a church that had few meetings and a lot of ministry?

Ponder these questions; they can help you pray about the focus of your church and your own call to ministry, and help you discern the will of the Spirit for what you will do next.

CHAPTER TWO

Growing Larger by Growing Smaller

Eddie Fox and George Morris were the two men responsible for the World Methodist Evangelism Conference in South Africa. They had invited Methodist Christians from all walks of life in the southern part of Africa to gather at a retreat center just outside of Johannesburg, South Africa. It was an ideal place for Christians to gather. It was here that I witnessed people who had a deep sense of joy in their lives. I discovered that the source of the joy that I witnessed in these people came from their strong walk with God. The vehicle for this movement of the Holy Spirit was not only worship but the weekly Wesley Class Meetings people attended. Wesley Class Meetings! I had read of John Wesley's small group movement in seminary. I was a lifelong Methodist and United Methodist, yet I had never heard of a Methodist church in recent years holding Wesley Class Meetings.

I began to ask questions about these Wesley Class Meetings. In most of the Methodist churches in South Africa, these class meetings of ten to fourteen people are conducted in much the same way as they were in John Wesley's day. During that week in South Africa I met Rowan Rogers, a pastor who specialized in organizing and overseeing the class meetings in his church. They were called Wesley Fellowship Groups, and every member of his church had to be in one. He was one of two pastors for the church, and his main responsibility was to ensure the ongoing work of the Wesley Fellowship Groups.

It was a leading of the Holy Spirit that caused me to ask Rowan, one afternoon while I was in South Africa, if he would pray about coming to Christ Church in Fort Lauderdale as a missionary. He and his wife, Liz, were invited to come for two years to teach us how to develop this unique kind of small group ministry.

Later that afternoon, I was surprised at myself for making such an offer without having any official approval. God was working in me without my really being aware of God's presence. Rowan said he would pray about the offer and asked me to contact him once I was back in Fort Lauderdale. Throughout my time in South Africa I saw more and more confirmation of the power of God being manifested through these Wesley Class Meetings.

When I returned to Fort Lauderdale, I knew something was changing in me; but I did not know exactly what it was. As mentioned in chapter 1, on my first Sunday back preaching, I asked the congregation to forgive my lack of spiritual leadership. The congregation's silence on that remark indicated that they didn't know what to think about it; it was as though I had just hiccuped and then went on with my message for the day.

As I thought about the congregation at Christ Church, I realized that the church was composed of good people who were doing what they had been taught for many years. For many of the members, being part of a church was as important as being a good citizen. Belonging to a church was something you did if you wanted to be a good person. I confess that my own ministry at Christ Church had helped foster that orientation to Christianity. Belonging to Christ Church for many people was like belonging to a club rather than to the church of Jesus Christ.

The general mind-set was of giving one hour a week to religious activity if you did not have anything better to do. This attitude was characteristic of people who were spiritually asleep. Seldom did I sense people yearning for the things of God. The people were like seeds planted in the soil, seeds that had never grown enough to blossom. They were good people who thought what they had was all there was to being a Christian.

Children were very important to our people. Parents would bring their children to Sunday school. While their children were in Sunday school, they would attend the 9:30 A.M. worship service. Thus that service came to have the best attendance, as people settled in there and got comfortable, having already taken their kids to Sunday school. It gave me the sense that being a member of the church was simply synonymous with being a good citizen, a good American. Church business meetings functioned much like the Rotary Club I had belonged to in another city. While there were exceptions, Christ Church was filled with what I would call "cultural Christians."

Cultural Christians, as I have come to understand the term, are people who have grown up thinking that all of their community was Christian. Since all are Christians, there is no need to share the gospel of Jesus Christ with others. Any attempt to do so would only steal people from another church. With a loss of the passion to win people to Jesus, cultural Christians fell into the gradual spiritual decline that happens when people lose the passion of their faith. Christianity was to be learned, not experienced. Christianity provided the ethical framework for all of life. One simply had to learn the right way to live. Part of living the right way meant being in worship from time to time. Cultural Christians subscribe to a kind of hen house logic: "If you sit in a hen house, it will make you a chicken." If you attend worship, you will be a Christian. Having a personal experience with Jesus Christ was replaced with simply attending worship. The cultural Christians I experienced in my years of ministry would find it difficult to distinguish between being a good citizen and being a Christian.

It had been so long since a commitment to Jesus had been preached that I knew I must begin there. (That is where God began with me in my own renewal.) I began to see my preaching as an invitation to become a follower of Jesus. This new style of preaching was accepted by most of the people. I must admit that I thought it strange to begin preaching basic Christianity to an established congregation. I started preaching as though I were speaking to a group of people who knew nothing about Christianity. I was calling our people to make a choice to be fully devoted followers of Jesus and to claim the new life that I knew God wanted for each of them. I was asking our people to make a decision for Jesus, to invite him into their lives, and to begin to experience the new life that I had begun to find while I was in South Africa.

Each Sunday I would preach basic Christianity with little outward response from the people. Few ever came forward at the end of the service when I issued the invitation to accept Jesus or to renew a commitment to Jesus. Nevertheless, I was faithful and continued to preach basic Christianity.

I had come to believe that there were not great crowds of our people who were fully devoted followers of Jesus. There were a small number of people who were deeply committed to Jesus. In the past I had tolerated them as people who were just a bit odd. These were the very people who were praying for me before I went to South Africa and continue praying for me to this present day. It was as if they knew that as I learned to walk with God, then the church would also grow into the body of Christ.

I am sure these wonderful people were praying for the

personnel committee to be responsive to what God was doing in my life. Because God is still active in redeeming the world, their prayers had a surprising effect on me and the personnel committee. I shared with the personnel committee the opportunity for us to invite Rowan Rogers and his wife to come as missionaries to us to teach of this unique small group ministry. There was a vacancy on our staff because one of our pastors had been reassigned to another church, and there had been a problem getting a pastor to fill his place. We were making progress getting another pastor when I suggested adding Rowan to the staff of the church. To my surprise the committee agreed and the invitation was issued.

What followed was an amazing work of God. Rowan and Liz had agreed to come, but they insisted on bringing their dog and cat. They began working on all the permits in October of 1991. They were to arrive in Fort Lauderdale in January of 1992. In August, a friend of mine informed me that the laws were changing the first of October. After that date it would be very difficult for a South African to come to the U.S.A. Normally it took about twelve weeks to process an application for a South African couple (including the pets) to come to the United States to work. Yet in only two weeks, Rowan and Liz's applications were completed and they were issued "green cards" that would allow them to work in the United States! To my way of thinking, it was simply an act of God that allowed the Rogers to be able to come.

The Rogers arrived in January of 1992, and Rowan began training leaders for Wesley Fellowship Groups the first week in February. With Rowan's help, a number of prospective leaders were recruited. Rowan held training sessions weekly for the next four weeks. Each prospective leader was to recruit his or her group. With a lot of effort twenty groups were started at the end of the leadership training. We would later discover that having the leader recruit the group was intentional and would give the groups something in common in addition to belonging to a Wesley Fellowship Group. To this day when we start a new group, the leader recruits the group. This gives each group its homogeneity or affinity. This key ingredient is the glue that keeps the groups together over a long period of time.

Principle 3

Growing larger by growing smaller.

This is a principle I should have known from reading the New Testament. Jesus set out to change the world by choosing a small group of people to disciple. Jesus did not start with the masses. He started with a small group of twelve people. John Wesley did the same with the Wesleyan movement in England. They were called Wesley Class Meetings. In the South African church, I discovered that this same small group ministry was still in practice. These groups from the South African Methodist Church, while particular to Methodism, contain principles that can easily be adapted to other non-Methodist traditions. The following is offered as a gift. I sincerely believe that Wesley Fellowship Groups were a gift from God and therefore come as a gift to you. Feel free to change the name, but know the principles are sound and important to growing people into fully devoted followers of Jesus.

WESLEY FELLOWSHIP GROUPS

They devoted themselves to the apostles' teaching and to the fellowship, to the breaking of bread and to prayer. . . . Every day they continued to meet together in the temple courts. They broke bread in their homes and ate together with glad and sincere hearts. (Acts 2:42-46 NIV)

In the early church there were no established church buildings. They met in small groups in homes. It was not until the third century that Christians began erecting buildings. With the advent of church buildings, the Christian community in general lost its small group dimensions.

John Wesley, the father of the Methodist movement, more than any other reformer helped reclaim the small group dynamic of church life. The Methodist renewal swept England with evangelistic fire that found its fundamental expression in small groups. There were three levels of groups in the Methodist movement:

1. United Societies: These were larger groups that met for prayer, exhortation, and mutual care.
2. Class Meetings: These were groups of ten to twelve people that met in homes and focused on the spiritual condition of each member.
3. Bands: These were smaller groups of five to eight persons of the same sex, designed to help foster deeper spiritual maturity.

At Christ Church our Wesley Fellowship Groups are modeled around the class meetings of John Wesley. They generally meet weekly in homes. The meetings usually last from one and a half to two hours in length. Groups are encouraged to leave an empty chair to remind them that each group is open to new people.

A TYPICAL NIGHT AT A WESLEY FELLOWSHIP GROUP

Twenty to thirty minutes of visiting for people to "catch up" with one another (snacks are often served)

Gathering for welcome, prayer, and introduction of new persons

Twenty to thirty minutes of sharing around the question: "How are you doing this week?"

Twenty to thirty minutes of Bible or topical study including group responses

Time of worship and closing prayers

Back to the snacks!

There are five essential ingredients in our Wesley Fellowship Group "recipe" that make these groups work. Every group finds its own proportion of the ingredients based on the group and individual needs and desires. When a group is new, it is important to keep in mind that all five ingredients will need to be in the life of the group. The ingredients are:

Fellowship. Fellowship meets our need to belong. In worship we often mingle, but seldom meet. Fellowship is the informal time where people get to know and love one another. This time usually happens as people gather. There will often be snacks.

Study. In the United States we have often confused Bible study with small groups. It is essential that each group studies the Bible. The study may be biblical (from Bible to life) or topical (life to Bible). The Bible is our "owners manual." Through the groups we seek to be a biblical people again. We believe that you grow people from where they are. This means that the leader and group choose the study material. Christ Church provides a sample copy of most small-group Bible study material that is published today. The group picks the material they would like to study, and each person pays for the study material. Some groups are using the most basic Bible study materials, while other groups are choosing more difficult biblical studies.

Accountability. The average church member does not feel comfortable being held accountable for his or her walk with God each week in a small group. We have found that in the first few months of a small group, people are more comfortable defining for the group what they want to be held accountable for in the next week. For example, if I were a member of a Wesley Fellowship Group, I might say to the group, "Please hold me accountable for reading the Bible each day this next week." The following week the group leader would ask me, "Dick, how did you do with reading your Bible this week?" I might respond, "Well, I read my Bible each day until I got to the weekend. I would like the group to hold me accountable for this area of my life again next week." As the group matures, the group and the leader can choose to agree upon a list of questions that each will answer for the past week. We all need help and accountability in our walk with God.

Worship and Prayer. It is important that each group have a time of worship and prayer. Sometimes singing a well-known hymn or praise chorus will lead a group into worship. Oftentimes a season of prayer is the worship time for groups. We try to ask all groups to close with a circle of prayer allowing each person an opportunity to pray.

Mission or Outreach. The journey inward must lead to the journey outward. Each group must find a time to be in mission or outreach. We feel that a group that focuses only on itself the whole time is like an ingrown toenail. It eventually brings pain to the whole body. Some groups will feed homeless people on a regular basis. Other groups will find some outreach ministry like helping build a Habitat for Humanity home. Each group is free to decide on the kind of outreach and frequency of that outreach. But each group must be in some way turning outward to help others. We need to give as well as receive.

WESLEY FELLOWSHIP GROUP LEADERS AND TRAINING

Currently we train Wesley Fellowship Group leaders in a three-hour session on a Sunday afternoon. Each

43

month there is a Sunday afternoon training session. We can do the training in three hours because most of our leaders now come out of existing Wesley Fellowship Groups. I have discovered that most people feel inadequate to the task of leading a Wesley Fellowship Group. We stress in the training session that a group leader is not a theologian like Karl Barth, a therapist like Sigmund Freud, or a leader like Moses. Wesley Fellowship Group leaders function more like facilitators than they do teachers. The group leader is to help the group and the individuals in the group to develop and grow as followers of Jesus. We say a group leader can be anyone who has:

A heart for God,
A love for people,
A resourceful mind,
Self-initiative, and
A commitment to small groups.

During this training session we spend some time helping potential leaders begin to understand the task and maintenance functions of a group leader. We have also found it helpful to provide some orientation to the life cycle of groups. We have adapted some material taken from *How to Lead Small Groups* by Neal F. McBride (Colorado Springs: NavPress, 1990). All groups have common cycles of growth and development regardless of the type of group or people in the group. Understanding these cycles is important for leaders of groups.

Phase 1: Birth and Infancy (first month)

The initial idea of beginning a group is conceived. The first meetings are held. The group is highly dependent on the leader during this stage.

44

Phase 2: Childhood (second month)

The group begins to form its own identity. Control of the group is an important issue now. A meeting format evolves.

Phase 3: Adolescence (third and fourth month)

A time of questioning develops as a few members complain about group meetings. The group is trying to decide how close they will come to one another. Leaders need to allow for questioning, recognizing that conflict is a necessary part of building close relationships.

Phase 4: Maturity and Multiplication (fifth through seventeenth months)

The group has taken on a life and energy of its own. It is accomplishing the purpose for which it was formed. Leaders need to maintain excitement and watch out for "midlife crisis." For the group to remain healthy, it must "launch" a new group. A new group is launched by one or two people from the group leaving to start another group. You will never want to divide the group in half. When this is done, usually both groups deteriorate and both groups die. We try to get each leader, before he or she starts a new group, to recruit an apprentice who agrees to leave the group during the maturity and multiplication stage and start a new group. By multiplying a group, we are not talking about splitting a group, but rather birthing a group. We say that your Wesley Fellowship Group is not "successful" until it is a grandparent—until it has birthed a new group, and then that group gives birth to a new group as well.

Phase 5: Old Age
(seventeenth through twenty-fourth months)

As this stage, the group will either redefine its purpose and gain new energy or it will lose members, interests, and eventually die. The task of the leader is to give the group a new vision and/or to recognize that the group needs to die gracefully.

I believe that when people are in a Wesley Fellowship Group, they are cared for and loved. In large-membership churches, people sometimes "fall through the cracks." Sometimes people have needs that the church staff simply misses. Much of the hurt that comes in local churches comes from not feeling that the church cares for you and about you. If you belong to a small group, you never are going to "fall through the cracks." You will be cared for and loved. You will also be able to care for and love the other people in your small group.

I saw this most clearly in the first year we began Wesley Fellowship Groups. I was aware of a couple who were very active in their Wesley Fellowship Group. His work took them up to West Palm Beach. They joined another church closer to their new home. He was doing some business in Fort Lauderdale and was suddenly taken ill and rushed to the hospital for emergency surgery. I got the call about 5:00 P.M. from his wife who was in the hospital waiting room. By the time I got to the hospital, it was around 5:30 P.M. By then all the members of the Wesley Fellowship Group they had belonged to were already there. The group members were caring for her and praying for him. While I was there, I observed this Wesley Fellowship Group also care for and pray for the other people who were waiting on loved ones in surgery. That small group stayed at the hospital until 11:00 P.M. that night. While I was there, I must admit I felt pretty useless as a pastor because the people in the small group were doing the ministry of Jesus! They did not need me, the professional pastor, to be in ministry that night. This was a powerful image of what I believe God intends for Christ Church. It is a goal to have all of the members of Christ Church in small groups. Someday we *will* have five hundred Wesley Fellowship Groups!

Currently, we ask all new members of the church to make a commitment to explore small groups by being in a Wesley Fellowship Group for six weeks. We find that about 98 percent of the people who try a Wesley Fellowship Group for six weeks will stay.

How long do we expect people to be in a Wesley Fellowship Group? As long as they walk with God. While it may not always be the same Wesley Fellowship Group, we believe that being in a small group is as important as being in worship each week.

Within six months of beginning our first twenty Wesley Fellowship Groups, I began to sense that God was doing a new thing at Christ Church. There was a movement of the Holy Spirit. As the leader, I now knew the direction in which God was leading our congregation. The most exciting days for Christ Church were just ahead of us.

FOR REFLECTION

1. Does your church have a focus on some kind of small-group ministry?

2. Do you sense that churches in the future will grow larger by growing smaller?

3. Do you feel there is value in people belonging to a small group to be discipled to Jesus?

4. Is this value equal to the value of people being in corporate worship each week?

CHAPTER THREE

New Wineskins for New Wine

And no one puts new wine into old wineskins. The wine would burst the wineskins, spilling the wine and ruining the skins. New wine needs new wineskins.
(Mark 2:2 NLT)

Since returning from South Africa in 1991, I have been praying in a different way. This new prayer has dramatically changed my life and ministry. I stopped praying for God to bless my clever ideas. I stopped asking God to fix the things I had started. Instead I prayed: **"Dear God, help me to be part of what you want to bless. Help our church to be part of what it is that you are blessing."**

This simple change in daily prayer has continually shifted my focus from me to God. Each day I pray that in this way it causes me to remember that I only participate in what it is God wants of me and of our church. What is happening at Christ Church must not be my clever thinking or coming up with a new fad. I must choose to surrender my will and be willing to choose to participate in what God is blessing.

The Wesley Fellowship Groups were evidence that God was doing a new thing at Christ Church. I wanted us to be part of what God was blessing. I was unsure of the direction the church was to go. I decided to go to our denominational retreat center in Florida for a week of prayer and fasting. I rented a room that had no television and no phone. I was to be alone with God that week.

Principle 4

Not my ideas, but a willingness to be part of what God is blessing.

During the week I asked God what it was that God wanted to bless at Christ Church and what it was that we were to do. Then I listened and listened and listened. I thought when I came back to the church I would have a thick theological document that would really impress people that I had been with God.

Instead, it was as if God said, "Dick, you are not all that bright, so I am going to make this really simple so that you don't get it all mixed up. I just want you and my people at Christ Church to do three things:

1. Introduce people to Jesus in positive ways
2. Disciple believers through Wesley Fellowship Groups
3. Relieve suffering."

I returned and shared with the staff what I thought to be God's vision for Christ Church. They confirmed what I had received as the direction for our church. I then shared this word from God with our lay leaders and then with the governing board of the church. I gave them a month to think and pray about it. The next month they adopted the vision I received while on retreat. But in order to know if this vision was really a word from God or just a clever attempt by my imagination to speak on God's behalf, I became convinced that I had to share the vision with the congregation for a year. I used the first three Sundays in January to outline the vision and then preached on the vision monthly for the next year. I continually tested this "vision" with the lay leadership of the church. At each meeting I renewed the proposal that this was what I felt God was asking of our church. I sampled people in informal ways to ask them if they felt this new vision was really what God wanted for our church.

At first people were somewhat indifferent to this new vision. I think many of the people I talked with felt that it would not harm anything, so it must be okay. But as the year moved along, I heard from laity in stronger and stronger ways that confirmed this new vision for Christ Church.

At the end of that year I knew what I received while on retreat was God's word for us. I had enough confirmation from the people of God at Christ Church to remove any doubt.

For us, we became more and more clear this was the "new wine" that Jesus spoke of in Mark 2:22. Old wineskins will not hold the "new wine" of Jesus. God was doing a new thing, and my prayer to be part of what God is blessing was beginning to come true.

My responsibility as the pastor was to lift this vision up before our people repeatedly. I began to ask each ministry area to justify what it was doing by the vision that God has given to Christ Church. Slowly but surely the ministries began to focus on God's vision for us. As a result, everything that happens at Christ Church must begin with prayer and justify itself in relation to God's vision for us.

My continuing task is to maintain the vision God has

given us. I must lift up the vision monthly in worship. Every new member must be able to say the vision from memory. It seems that the natural tendency of groups like our church is to blur the focus as time goes by. Therefore, my responsibility is to keep the vision as the driving focus for Christ Church. It is a task that has no end.

In January 1992 very little of our church organization was functioning according to this new vision God had given us. I spent all my time attending meetings. There were so many meetings that I believe the laity actually thought ministry was nothing more than meetings!

I knew in my heart that this was not the way a church was supposed to function. I used these meetings to share and test this new vision for our church. If nothing else, all these meetings provided time for input from the laity about the proposed vision for our church.

My denomination had structured itself and our churches to be governed and led by committees. My guess is that the denomination was fearful of a misuse of power. So, the thinking must have been, "if most of the power rests in groups of people, then the misuse of power can be minimized." This led to the conclusion that there must be a committee for every good cause. The necessity for leadership was placed on the back burner of church organization. The result was a congregation that had wandered away from the New Testament understanding of the church. Many of our churches are filled with good pastors and good people trying to follow their denominational guidelines. In the meantime, our numbers are falling and much of what is done is simply the "rearranging of deck chairs on the Titanic."

Since what my denomination gave me no longer worked, I decided to look to the future by looking to the past.

Principle 5

The Bible is the best source for what the church needs to be.

As I read the New Testament, I could find only one place where the voting majority ruled. That was in Acts 27. Paul had instructed the crew not to set sail. The crew decided what to do by a majority vote.

> *And since the harbour was unsuitable for wintering, the majority were for putting out from there in the hope of wintering at Phoenix—a harbour in Crete, facing south-west and north-west.*
> *A southerly breeze sprang up and, thinking their objective as good as reached, they weighed anchor and began to sail past Crete, close inshore.*
> *(Acts 27:12-13 NJB, emphasis added)*

The result was that the boat sank.

> *But the cross-currents carried them into a shoal and the vessel ran aground. The bows were wedged in and stuck fast, while the stern began to break up with the pounding of the waves.*   *(Acts 27:41 NJB)*

This is the only account I could find in the New Testament of decision making by democratic vote. I began to realize that neither my opinion, nor that of the committees of the church, matters. The only thing that really matters is the will of God.

I believe the church was never meant to be a democracy. We in the church are to function under a theocracy. The only thing that matters is the will of God. We must use prayer and Scripture as the tools to help us discern the will of God for our church.

I presented this notion about not voting to the governing

body at Christ Church for three months in a row. At the fourth month I simply said, "I don't think we can vote anymore if we are to be God's church." Others agreed and we quit voting. We decided that if an activity focuses on our vision statement and is supported by Scripture, then those proposing the new ministry could begin. No vote is needed when you realize that God's will is all that matters.

We best discern God's desire by looking to Scripture. God is amazingly consistent. If something is God's will—caring for the poor, for example—then it will be supported in Scripture. I need to see if the decision we are making is based on principles found in Scripture. I need to know if there are people willing to do this ministry. Has someone felt called to do this particular thing? Does the ministry fit into the broad vision that we believe God has given to our church? Will God have to do a miracle for this ministry to happen? (In other words, is this ministry larger than we can do?) If we can answer in the affirmative to these questions, then it is time to pray to see if we feel some leading from God or some concern that would come from God that would cause us to wait or to reject the proposed ministry. The following account illustrates how we discerned God's will, in this case when a group that was not part of our church requested to use our facilities.

We were presented with a request by an interfaith ministry group, led by Arnold Abbot, called Love Thy Neighbor. They had been using a synagogue to prepare food to feed homeless people in Broward County, but they had just been asked to seek another base of operations. We had recently completed a new building on the Christ Church campus with a commercially equipped kitchen. Arnold wanted to know if his group could use our new kitchen to prepare food for about four hundred homeless people each Wednesday during the summer, until he could find another place for his ministry.

That request was brought to the governing body of our church. All the details had been worked out with Arnold

53

and some of the Christ Church staff. The question was: "Could this group use our kitchen each Wednesday for the summer?" Given that we were committed not to vote, how could we decide on this activity by an outside group?

The governing body understood that this ministry fit God's vision for our church (to relieve suffering). It was biblical to feed the hungry. It did not matter what any of us thought about this issue. The only thing that mattered was whether this was God's will for our church.

I asked the governing body to pray in silence for the next ten minutes and to try to discern any word from God that would be a signal to wait or a signal not to allow this ministry to use our facilities. What was God's will in this issue? As people bowed their heads for this ten minutes of silent prayer, I could see some of the people thinking, "We are going to pray at our governing body meeting?"

If you have not been accustomed to having silent prayer, then ten minutes is a long time. After ten minutes I asked if anyone had a word from God that would be a negative, a concern, or a "not now" that the group should hear. There was silence except for one person. This person said, "As I was praying, I heard God saying to me that we should not let this feeding ministry use our kitchen for the summer, but all year—as long as they need our kitchen."

Hearing no other word from God, I suggested that since no one heard a negative or any other concerns, we would assume that God wanted Love Thy Neighbor to use our church kitchen each Wednesday as long as they needed it. The group has been using our kitchen for three years now, and it adds a wonderful dimension to our ministries.

Love Thy Neighbor often prepares additional food to assist with our own feeding ministry on Thursday night. Each Wednesday and Thursday, anywhere from two hundred to eight hundred hungry people are fed with food prepared in the kitchen at Christ Church.

In a democracy, our governing body would have framed the question as whether this outside group should use our church kitchen. If that were how we had approached this decision and if we had taken the customary vote on it, I am certain that we would have stood a good chance of doing our will rather than the will of God. Sometimes the denomination requires us to vote and the State of Florida requires that the trustees be elected. But as far as possible we are trying to discern the will of God and act on that will without resorting to democratic vote, through which so often our desire to be in charge can prevent us from truly discerning what God wants us to do.

Remember Principle 2

God honors obedience.

My task is to help our congregation understand that being obedient (faithful) followers of Jesus is *the call* for us in life. God will honor and bless obedience. I understand obedience as choosing to seek and discern the will of God as a follower of Jesus. The more we as a congregation can learn to choose obedience and faithfulness, the more God blesses and honors our efforts. God's blessings do not mean everything always gets larger and larger. But when a church is receiving God's blessings, everything is better. The question then becomes: "If we seek obedience to the will of God, how should we go about organizing our life together?"

Principle 6

Form follows function.

The direction was clear. As listed above, we as a church were to:

1. Introduce people to Jesus in positive ways
2. Disciple believers through Wesley Fellowship Groups
3. Relieve suffering

Now we needed a "new wineskin" for the "new wine." To go forward I felt we must look backward to see how the church was organized according to the New Testament. As I looked at the New Testament, I found three images that would help us as a church to live into what God was doing in our midst.

1. The church is a "fellowship."

They devoted themselves to the apostles' teaching and fellowship, *to the breaking of bread and the prayers.*
(Acts 2:42 NRSV, emphasis added)

Fellowship is best characterized by unity. Unity is what God wants for us in order to be part of what God is blessing. As the people at Christ Church came to realize that we were to be about only the three values God had given to us, it became easier to move to that kind of unity. Our decision to become a theocracy instead of a democracy was a good one. Voting creates winners and losers. The very act of voting undermines the unity God desires for God's church. Every time there is a vote there is a great potential to undermine the unity of the church. Voting also focuses on what we think and want. It tends to take the focus away from discerning the will of God.

The movement of our congregation toward Wesley Fellowship Groups is to see that the way to grow larger is to grow smaller. The very nature of the Wesley Fellowship Groups underscores that all people have a need to know and be known. When the day comes that all our people are in Wesley Fellowship Groups, we will have attained the unity that God intends for a local church.

We are learning that being in a small group is just as important as being in worship each week. We expect people to be in a Wesley Fellowship Group as long as they walk with God.

It is amazing to see that as God's Spirit begins to come alive in a congregation, there is more love and unity. As individuals begin to grow spiritually and the "fruits of the spirit" increase, there is more love and unity in the local congregation. And when there are differences, solutions can be found without people getting angry and leaving.

2. The church is a "body."

Now there are varieties of gifts, but the same Spirit; and there are varieties of services, but the same Lord; and there are varieties of activities, but it is the same God who activates all of them in everyone. To each is given the manifestation of the Spirit for the common good. To one is given through the Spirit the utterance of wisdom, and to another the utterance of knowledge according to the same Spirit, to another faith by the same Spirit, to another gifts of healing by the one Spirit, to another the working of miracles, to another prophecy, to another the discernment of spirits, to another various kinds of tongues, to another the interpretation of tongues. All these are activated by one and the same Spirit, who allots to each one individually just as the Spirit chooses.

For just as the body is one and has many members, and all the members of the body, though many, are one body, so it is with Christ. For in the one Spirit we were all baptized into one body—Jews or Greeks, slaves or free—and we were all made to drink of one Spirit.

Indeed, the body does not consist of one member but of many. If the foot would say, "Because I am not a hand, I do not belong to the body," that would not make it any less a part of the body. And if the ear would say, "Because I am not an eye, I do not belong to the body," that would not make it any less a part of the body. If the whole body were an eye, where would the hearing be? If the whole body were hearing, where would the sense of smell be? But as it is, God arranged the members in the body, each one of them, as he chose. If all were a single member, where would the body be? As it is, there are many members, yet one body. The eye cannot say to the hand, "I have no need of you," nor again the head to the feet, "I have no need of you." On the contrary, the members of the body that seem to be weaker are indispensable, and those members of the body that we think less honorable we clothe with greater honor, and our less respectable members are treated with greater respect; whereas our more respectable members do not need this. But God has so arranged the body, giving the greater honor to the inferior member, that there may be no dissension within the body, but the members may have the same care for one another. If one member suffers, all suffer together with it; if one member is honored, all rejoice together with it. Now you are the body of Christ and individually members of it.

(1 Corinthians 12:4-27 NRSV)

Could it be that God wants to view the church not as an organization or business that needs to be kept and maintained, but rather as a "body" equipped on the basis of spiritual gifts? I believe this is exactly how God wants to view the church.

Rather than having elected officers, I believe the biblical way is for the church to function on the basis of spiritual gifts. As people begin to know and understand the spiritual gifts that God gives, each person finds a place of ministry that fits his or her own spiritual gifts. We are beginning to use "Network," provided by the Willow Creek Church, as a way to help people discover and claim their spiritual gifts. Someday all our people will be in ministry on the basis of their spiritual gifts.

Just as a body is composed of different parts, such as foot, finger, shoulder, and so forth, so too the Body of Christ is to be composed of smaller groups of people who help the body be whole, healthy, fit, and complete. This would mean that the church would be divided into smaller groups of people for study and fellowship (Wesley Fellowship Groups). Other groups would do ministry according to their spiritual gifts (Prison Ministry, Ushers, Homeless Ministry, Youth Ministry, and so forth). As is true in our physical bodies, these smaller groups tend to operate on the basis of relationships rather than rules.

Principle 7

The greater the relationship, the fewer the rules.

When Eileen and I were first married, I was surprised to find out there were so many rules. There were rules about where to squeeze the toothpaste tube, rules about picking up one's dirty clothes, rules about how you wash dishes, rules about taking out the trash, and on and on. Now after thirty-three years of marriage we have only one rule in our family. That rule is to always tell the truth. Everything else is based on relationship. The greater the relationship, the fewer the rules. Can our church feel and operate like the Body of Christ when there are few rules? I believe that the answer is Yes! If a church can be clear about what it is that God is blessing, and move as a theocracy (not a democracy), then I believe we can move closer to enhanced relationships and fewer rules.

Most of the time rules come about because someone makes a mistake, and a rule is put in place to ensure that other people don't make the same mistake. If we can begin to realize the common vision in any church, then God's work in our midst is to grow our relationships with God and each other. The result at Christ Church has been far fewer rules than there were ten years ago.

3. The church is a "flock."

Here's my concern: that you care for God's flock with all the diligence of a shepherd. Not because you have to, but because you want to please God. Not calculating what you can get out of it, but acting spontaneously. Not bossily telling others what to do, but tenderly showing them the way.

When God, who is the best shepherd of all, comes out in the open with his rule, he'll see that you've done it right and commend you lavishly.   (1 Peter 5:2-4 *The Message*)

As I read John 10:14, where Jesus says "I am the good shepherd; I know my sheep and my sheep know me" (NIV), it became clear that Jesus was not advocating caring for sheep (flock) by committee. In fact one of Jesus' favorite words is *shepherd.* I began to see Christ Church as a number of flocks that would need leadership and care by more than one or two shepherds (pastors). First Peter 5:2-4 is a wonderful image of the work of shepherds in the life of a church. I began to sense the need to let God raise up Lay Pastors to care for and lead the ministries of Christ Church. In June 1994 I began to consecrate Lay Pastors, of whom we now have more than one hundred.

Lay Pastors at Christ Church fit into three categories:

1. *Wesley Fellowship Group Leaders.* Wesley Groups meet each week for one or two hours. The very nature of a Wesley Fellowship Group makes each Wesley Fellowship Group leader a logical person to be a Lay Pastor. The leader of the Wesley Fellowship Group is the shepherd of that small group of people.

2. *Administrative Groups* (Finance Committee, Trustees,

and other similar groups). Each of these groups is led by a Lay Pastor. Administrative groups need to be seen as ministry and not business. These Lay Pastors are the spiritual leaders for their action group in the church.

3. *Action Ministries.* These are groups like Ushers, Clothing Ministry, Prison Ministry, Choirs, Feeding Ministry, and so on. Each group that meets at least once a month will have a Lay Pastor. The work of a Lay Pastor or Lay Shepherd is to be the leader and the basic caregiving person for his or her group.

Any person who leads a ministry can be a Lay Pastor. Any person who is a member of the church and is called by God can be a Lay Pastor. Lay Pastors are not chosen by the church or by the pastor of the church, but they are called by God. A person who feels called by God meets with one of the ordained pastors of the church. If the call fits within God's vision for our church, that person is invited to be a Lay Pastor.

There are four simple requirements that all Lay Pastors agree to follow. **The first requirement is that each Lay Pastor must commit to a daily time of prayer and Scripture reading.**

Principle 8

You cannot share what you do not have.

Lay Pastors need to keep spiritually focused. This daily time will allow the Lay Pastors to pray for the church and especially for the people for whom the Lay Pastor is responsible. It takes time to grow one's relationship with God. I believe we must walk daily with God. All of our Lay Pastors understand this.

The second requirement is that each Lay Pastor be spiritually focused with intentionality in his or her

area of ministry. Lay Pastors are to spend at least some of their time getting their group together for prayer before they actually begin their work. It could be as little as ten minutes. The Lay Pastor is to gather the group and look spiritually at how each person's week has been since they last met. Lay Pastors are to note any concerns of the group and remind them that each person pray for the other members during the following week. Then each Lay Pastor is to invite the group to be in prayer for their ministry. This seems to work best if people join hands and each person is invited to say a brief prayer, moving around the circle. If someone does not feel comfortable when praying out loud, the person can simply squeeze the hand of the person next to him or her and pass. I am told that this requirement is very similar to early Methodist Class Meetings and other intentional groups of shared discipleship throughout Christian history.

The third requirement is to fill out a brief form each month so that the church office knows who has been added or who has left that ministry area. There is also a place on the form to note any prayer requests or problems the ministry group is having.

The fourth requirement is the monthly training of Lay Pastors. We call it "L.I.G.H.T." It stands for Laity In God's Holy Training. Lay Pastors meet the second Sunday of each month at 5:00 P.M. Everyone is welcome to the LIGHT meeting. Spouses are welcome. Friends are welcome. Church members are welcome. Anyone is welcome to come and be part of the LIGHT meeting the second Sunday of each month. All Lay Pastors must be present. Only when a Lay Pastor is out of town or suffering an illness does that Lay Pastor have an adequate reason for missing LIGHT meeting. If a Lay Pastor misses for other reasons, that person cannot continue as a Lay Pastor. It is my responsibility to see that the Lay Pastors are spiritually fed, trained, encouraged, and equipped to lead in their ministry area. Carl Sallade is a Lay Pastor who gave his

World Series ticket to another person because he knew that his first priority was to be at the LIGHT meeting. Being a Lay Pastor comes with a cost!

Lay Pastors will be added as God calls us into new Action Ministries and as we begin new Wesley Fellowship Groups. We consecrate new Lay Pastors every few months. This is an ongoing process. Lay Pastors are the basic caregivers of the congregation. All of our ministry groups are small enough that the Lay Pastor notices when someone is troubled or someone is absent. I was surprised to find Lay Pastors making hospital calls. I went to visit a person many people know and love in our congregation. When I asked to see the person, the nurse asked who I was. I said, "I'm Dick Wills, one of the pastors of Christ Church." She looked at me and said, "There have been about twenty people in here to see the person, and they all say they are a pastor of Christ Church." I said, "Well, that's right; we are all pastors." I knew from that moment I had to use my next monthly Lay Pastor Training Meeting to teach about how one makes hospital calls as a Lay Pastor!

When there are so many pastors (lay and ordained) in a church, what is my role as a pastor? Am I always in charge of everything? I am learning that God honors shared leadership.

Principle 9

God honors shared leadership.

When I participate in a ministry that is led by a Lay Pastor, I am simply one of the members of that ministry. I am there under the authority and leadership of that Lay Pastor. When I participate in our homeless feeding ministry, the Lay Pastor is in charge. She tells me what I am to do. Some weeks I get to serve macaroni. Other weeks she has me fold napkins and hand out plastic spoons, forks, and plates. I really love it when I get to serve macaroni. I hate it when she tells me to fold those napkins and hand out plastic spoons, forks, and plates. But I simply do what I am asked because I submit myself to her authority as the Lay Pastor of homeless feeding. Sometimes the Lay Pastor will ask me to go out and visit with a troubled homeless person. It is a shared leadership in the Body of Christ that God honors and blesses.

As Christ Church becomes a more biblical church, I am finding the Holy Spirit is touching lives I could have never touched on my own. No new system, no new management style, no new denominational organization can do what the work of the Holy Spirit does and is doing once I, the pastor, have chosen to be obedient and have begun to trust God. There are new wineskins for the new wine. You can see it and feel it these days at our church. We are beginning to become what we understand to be a New Testament church. And God is very good!

FOR REFLECTION

1. As you read the New Testament, are there some images that would help you see a new way of being a local church?

2. Is there unity of purpose in your church?

3. Have you found meaningful biblical ways of empowering laypersons?

4. Would lay pastors be a possibility in your local church?

5. Could you begin to think and pray about releasing laypersons for shared leadership in your church?

6. Would you be willing to have accountability for your life and ministry as well as to have laypersons who have been called by God to lead ministries?

CHAPTER FOUR

Trusting God Enough Not to Be Loved by Everybody

I am always bothered when people do not like me. I guess I was raised to try to please people. It is my observation over thirty years of ministry that a lot of pastors are just like me in wanting to please the people in the church. Over the years I have done so much to try to make people in the church happy, but it has been mostly a "no win" situation. I just don't seem to be able to make all the people happy all the time. As I have thought about this, I think I am learning that what I really wanted from the people in the church was to be loved. The ways I have practiced ministry have been to get people to love me. In the past six years I have decided that is the wrong place for a pastor like me to be.

It is spiritually draining to live your life trying to make everyone happy in order to get them to love you. I suspect that my weariness in 1991 was due to having spent so many years trying to make people happy, with the assumption that if they were happy, they would love me. I probably have a strong streak of codependency in my personality. I really would like everyone to be happy and to love me!

What I needed was to know that I was loved by God. I had been looking to the people for that love when all along God was there trying to offer God's love to me. The more I am aware of God's love for me, the less I live my life trying to please people. I am learning that I am to be a channel of God's love to others. There is no way I can have all the love it takes to be the pastor of a church. I must let God shape me and fill me so that I can love people in the same way Jesus loves me.

I picture the shaping God is doing in my life as a heart. Early in my Christian walk I experienced God's love through Jesus. God was taking my shapeless mass and molding me into the image of a heart. The first step was to rub off the rough edges. That was not all that bad, after all I liked being a heart. But then God began to push this new "heart" in ways I don't like. For example, I am supposed to love my enemies. I am supposed to grow my relationship with God. I am to value people who are different. I am supposed to love the unlovely. I don't like all this pushing God is doing with my new "heart." It feels like I will lose a lot, for God is hollowing out this new heart. Much of this process is very painful to me.

Finally I have begun to realize that I don't have the ability to love all the people all the time. I don't have enough love in my life to do that. This is why God has to hollow out my heart, in order to make me a vessel of God's love. God has plenty of love for all kinds of people, including me. My call into the ministry has been an ongoing shaping of my life so that I can be a channel of God's love to others. I don't always like the pain of having God poke here and there in my new heart, but I am learning that it is always good. I am learning that obedience to God is a choice that I can make. It is here that I am learning that important principle.

Again remember Principle 2

God honors and blesses obedience.

The more I am willing to choose to be obedient to what I know of God's will, the less I spend my life trying to please all the people all the time. I have learned, however, that this produces some painful moments when people choose to leave our church because I cannot please them.

I remember a man who I really admired. He was a man of position, wealth, and power. We were friends. In late fall one year he came to me and said that he and his family would be leaving our church to go to another church in our community. When I asked why, he said, "I just don't like the new music you are doing at the 9:30 A.M. service. I was raised in another denomination, and I have decided to return to my roots." I said to my friend, "Why don't you and your family come to the 11:00 A.M. service because it is exactly what you have been having at the 9:30 A.M. service before we shifted some of the music?" He replied, "I can't. I have a tee-off time at 12:00 noon each Sunday." I said, "If it meant that with this new kind of music we could reach people who are hurting and live in great darkness and brokenness and share with them the love of Jesus, would you be willing to shift your tee-time 15 minutes to 12:15 P.M.?" I will never forget his simple reply, "Hell, no!"

I felt like weeping. He was a very good friend, and I really wanted him to be happy. A short time later he and his family went to another church where the music was exactly to his liking at the 9:30 A.M. service.

It is difficult to have people you really care about choose another church because you cannot or will not try to please them. So many Christians appear to have settled for so much less than a New Testament faith. The ongoing question of many church members is "What are you going to do for me?" Often there is little evidence of members of a local church wanting to know how they can give their lives away for the sake of Jesus. I believe evil triumphs when good church members end up wanting the church to cater to them.

For many of us the church has grown full of what Bill Hybels calls "neutralized Christians." Hybels writes:

> He (Satan) tries to *neutralize* our faith. He does this by convincing sincere young believers that their new and boundless enthusiasm is nothing more than a manifestation of spiritual adolescence which *will* and *should* fade with age. He likewise convinces more mature believers that they should demonstrate their spiritual maturity by living serious, predictable, semi-sedated Christian lives that attest to their "quiet consistency." In short, he tries to dupe you into "mellowing out" and "settling in" to a powerless, watered-down, neutralized Christian existence. (*Christians in the Marketplace* [Wheaton, Ill.: Victor Books, 1982], 131)

Similarly, Chad Walsh writes:

> Millions of Christians live in sentimental haze of vague piety with soft organ music trembling in the lovely light from stained glass windows. Their religion is a pleasant thing of emotional quivers, divorced from the will, divorced from the intellect and demanding little except lip service to a few harmless platitudes. I suspect that Satan has called off his attempt to convert people to agnosticism. After all, if a man travels far enough away from Christianity, he is liable to see it in perspective and decide it is true. It is much safer from Satan's point of view, to vaccinate a man with a mild case of Christianity so as to protect him from the real disease. (*Early Christians of the Twenty-first Century* [Westport, Conn.: Greenwood Press, 1972], 11)

Sadly a lot of churches have bought into having a comfortable, pseudo-Christian mind-set. The result is that churches that should be strong and vital in introducing

people to Jesus and making these new people fully committed disciples of Jesus are trying to please the people
who have joined with only a token interest in people who
live in darkness and brokenness. No wonder church leaders are saying that 80 percent of the churches in the United
States are static or declining.

What has happened has been a failure of leadership. My
friend was leaving our church because other pastors and I
had tried to please him and make him comfortable. We had
not invited him to commit his life to Jesus and to journey
toward being a fully committed disciple who would be willing to give up anything to bring new people into a relationship with Jesus. I think somewhere along the way we had
just wanted to please our people, do a good job, and be loved.

I am learning that obedience is to choose daily to give
my life to God. Obedience is a journey of walking with
Jesus each day so that my life becomes more and more an
expression of Jesus to the world. John Ortberg has para-
phrased Luke 6:40 this way: "My ultimate goal in life is to
live as Jesus would live if he were in my place."

It is that obedience that God honors and blesses. This
means a daily walk with God that more and more leads me
to live a surrendered life. I have to give up trying to control
the ministries of God's church. I have to give up my fancy
ideas. I have to give up my little thinking about the way I
would like the church to be. I have to give up everything
except a tenacious desire to do the will of God. It really
does not matter what I think. It only matters what is the
will of God. This is why each day I pray for God to help me
be part of what God is blessing.

*Trust in the LORD with all your heart and lean not on
your own understanding.* (Proverbs 3:5 NIV)

The amazing discovery for me has been that the more I
surrender my life, the less afraid I am of not pleasing people. My tears continue to flow when people leave the

church or don't understand. But more and more I am filled only with sadness when people choose to be comfortable over choosing to be faithful, rather than feeling that I have failed to make them happy and hence make them love me.

The journey is learning to be obedient and to trust God. This has meant that I really don't know where the church is going. Wonderful laypeople keep saying to me, "Dick, what is the plan?" I tell them "I don't know. But I want to stay close to the One who does know and do whatever God wants us to do." As the church has grown and developed over the past six years, it is obvious that there is a plan and reason for all that has happened. I take no credit for any of what God has done in our church. It has all been a gift to me, and I share that gift with anyone who has an interest.

Trusting God is about faith. It is about finding comfort in not being able to see the future at the moment. Robert E. Quinn has described this trust as building a bridge as you walk on it (*Deep Change: Discovering the Leader Within* [San Francisco: Jossey-Bass Publishers, 1996], 83). When God gives you a vision of what can be and will be with faith and trust in God, it almost certainly does not mean that the leader will have a plan. This is where trusting in God comes in. We are to walk by faith, not by sight.

> *For we walk by faith, not by sight.*
> (2 Corinthians 5:7 NRSV)

The world in which we live always wants things well planned in advance. Most of us really don't want to trust God for the future. We would rather have a plan and do it ourselves. This usually means that we will be worn out by the weariness of doing good.

Trusting is really like building a bridge as you walk on it. You do not know where it is going or how long the bridge will be when you are finished. I am finding that as I trust God and grow in the desire only to be part of what God is blessing, I am not afraid as much and am given loving courage to continue to follow. I trust God to provide the necessary resources and people at the right time.

I remember reading that when Gandhi was working in South Africa, he had a vision of what he was to do. One day, a man arrived from another country and volunteered to join Gandhi. The man asked, "Aren't you surprised that I have come here to work with you?" "No," Gandhi replied. He pointed out that when one discovers what is right and begins to pursue it, the necessary people and resources tend to present themselves.

That has been exactly my experience these past six years at the church I serve. The right people and the right resources appear always in God's timing and that timing is always the best. With all the different kinds of music we do each weekend, it has been a stretch to find musicians who can lead in various types of worship that we now require. I remember that we began our contemporary praise service with one guitar player. God sent other people to us as we prayed about this matter. Of course, I wanted the people much sooner, but God's timing of these people was perfect. Torri Barnette had been a backup singer to Gloria Estefen. When she came to Christ Church, although she looked great on the outside, the inside was broken. She was divorced and an alcoholic who did not feel worthy to be in any church. One Sunday Jesus met Torri in our service, and she was given a brand new life. She began singing with our Praise Band. Soon she became the Lay Pastor leading the worship in three of our five weekend services.

Tony Chance is a local celebrity in our community with a long history here as a nightclub entertainer. He came to our church because one of our members invited him to come. Something of the spirit of Jesus touched Tony, and he came back a second time. It wasn't long before Jesus was giving Tony a brand new life. Tony shared his testimony in church one Easter Sunday. Like Torri's, it was a true story of the power of the Resurrection and what Jesus can do in single life. Since that time Tony has felt a call to ministry and is going for a month each summer to seminary. Tony has recently been named as the Pastor of Worship and Music at our church. My denomination has given approval for him to be appointed to our church as one of the pastors. I am convinced that God was active in redeeming both Torri and Tony, and they were at our church at just the right time.

There are pastors who tell me that they do not believe God is still active in the lives of people. They say, "What God did in Jesus was the complete work of God. Now it is only up to us to follow the teachings of Jesus." I understand this position because for many years my ministry functioned on just this assumption. I did religious work, but most of the time I was acting out of my own energy. Since 1991 I have begun to experience a God who is active in redeeming the world. Usually God waits for my willingness to be a vehicle for God's will and purpose. I have witnessed so many changed lives in the past six years that no one could convince me that God is not actively involved trying to redeem the whole world.

There are and continue to be people who stay and yet want to be appeased. We must not blame these people. They are the product of what pastors have taught people about the church. When your source of love is from God, then it is easier to love these people even though they are clearly not happy with you. You will learn to pray daily for such folks and to ask God to fill the emptiness in their lives. God will give you the gift of loving each of these persons if you continue to pray God's best blessings for them. You will have the gift of loving even the hardest to love in your congregation. I know because I have seen God give me that love for people in the church I serve.

If you are a pastor or layperson who doesn't believe that God is active in the world today, you will find this book disturbing. You may rationalize that Dick has gone off the deep end. You will focus on the model of Christ Church. You will think, "If I just get Wesley Fellowship Groups started and use Lay Pastors, then my church will be as vital and loving as Christ Church." If you only look to the model of our church, I believe that you will be deeply disappointed in efforts to duplicate what God has done and is doing at Christ Church.

If you do not believe that God is active in the world today, you will want people to love you. You will be disappointed with yourself because the cost of trying to get people to love you is very high. You will get stuck doing religious things that more and more will seem empty. This is because Christianity is about a relationship not a religion. You will try to change the world by doing good things for the community. It will tend to use you up because you do not walk daily with the God who is still active in the world today. You will find that it is more and more difficult to act as a person with great courage in the face of the forces of evil in our time.

A daily walk with God is the way to grow your relationship with the God who became flesh in Jesus. The greater that relationship, the more love and courage will fill your life. You will grow less and less afraid. You will grow stronger in doing the things of God and become less bound to pleasing people. You will know that you are loved by God in Jesus and find that freedom to live as one of the disciples of Jesus.

"The thief comes only to steal and kill and destroy. I have come so that they may have life and have it to the full." (John 10:10 NJB)

The biblical promise is that your life will be full. No longer are you dependent on people to determine who you are and whose you are. When you are trusting God and walking daily with God, you will have a growing courage to do what God places before you.

More and more I have been released from trying to please all the people in my·church. This does not mean that I am free to do whatever I want. Nor does it mean that my heart does not break when someone leaves because our church is changing to reach non-Christians. When you choose to be obedient and to live with great love, you will suffer. If Jesus suffered because he loved and called people to a right relationship with God, then realistically you and I can expect the same thing to happen to us. You cannot be faithful to God and not suffer. But the promise is real. The life that Jesus promises his followers is full indeed!

FOR REFLECTION

1. Do you trust God enough not to be loved by everybody?

2. Do you trust God enough to love those who do not love you?

3. Is God shaping your life so that you will have a greater capacity to love?

CHAPTER FIVE

The Main Focus: Becoming a Spiritual Leader

To be a vital church for the new century a church will need indigenous worship, small groups, and the empowerment of the laity.

Indigenous worship simply means the church will provide worship that will connect people with God. It is important to understand the people who live in your community, especially those who are unchurched. There does not seem to be any indication that the future will hold up any one form of worship that will be for all people. Most churches will probably provide a variety of worship styles for the different groups of people within their community. There are all kinds of educational experiences being offered to help churches find the worship styles appropriate for their community.

In the years to come churches will grow larger by growing smaller. Small groups will be the core and foundation of vital churches. We are blessed with a large variety of options for small group models that are designed for the local church. In almost every church periodical there is some offering of a small group structure for the local church.

To embrace a new century, churches will learn ways to empower laity. The laity are a largely untapped reservoir of talent and person power that will enable the church to be a vital force in the world. Clergy and laity will work together in doing the work of Jesus in our broken world. Almost every denomination has a plan for the empowerment of the laity for the future.

One might think that if a church has indigenous worship, small groups, and empowerment of the laity, it will certainly be a vital community of faith. But there is a problem. The fundamental need is for the pastor to be a "spiritual leader." The problem is this: **There are few models in the mainline churches of spiritual leaders.**

Most pastors need models to guide them in the development of becoming a spiritual leader of a local church. Over the years the church has gravitated to the secular world for its understanding of leadership models. In my own lifetime I have had wonderful church leaders model their particular style of leadership. There have been leaders who were managers. There have been leaders who were CEOs. There have been leaders who were innovators. There have been leaders who were charismatic and who could get people to follow them anywhere. But there have been few spiritual leaders that served as models for pastors. The result of not having spiritual leaders has been at least part of the reason for the decay of the church in recent history.

Too often pastors and churches die a slow death. What is needed is deep spiritual change in the lives of pastors so that pastors can become the spiritual leaders that God needs. The church will never experience renewal without spiritual leaders. For people like me what was needed was deep spiritual change so that I might become the spiritual leader that God called me to be.

Principle 10

Individual change precedes organizational change.

For most pastors the choice is deep spiritual change or a slow death. How do you know if you or your church is dying? Below are eight areas to explore to help you determine if you or your church is dying a slow death. Ask yourself if any of these are true of you or your church:

- You or the church values conservative decisions (You don't spend money, don't take risks, etc.);
- You avoid deep spiritual change;
- You explain away or ignore external criticism;
- There are only short-term, day-to-day operating procedures (no clear and compelling vision of what can be and will be with faith in God);
- The pastor and leaders focus on management, not leadership;
- People have a sense of hopelessness;
- There are needed changes that no one is willing to make;
- Failure to make needed changes is undiscussable.

The question then is, *"Are you or your church dying a slow death?"* As a pastor or leader there are at least three options:

Peace at any price. This means you don't "rock the boat." Leave things as they are. Don't upset anyone. Keep trying to please all the people all the time. When this happens something precious in you dies. I know because it happened to me before I went to South Africa.

Exit. You leave. In some denominational systems it means the pastor asks the denominational executive to work out a move to another church. In other denominational systems the pastor begins to look for churches that need a pastor to employ. The pastor may begin circulating his or her name through the denominational channels, falling victim to the old lie that "The grass always looks greener on the other side of the hill." If a pastor is older, he or she explores the option of retirement. Doing nothing seems a better option than dying a slow death in the church you serve now. And for some the pain is so great that these pastors simply exit from the ministry. I am told that the exit rate among clergy is very high. I know that of the thirty pastors ordained with me in 1965 only three of us are still in our geographical area and active in ministry today. I don't think anyone really knows the heartache and pain of dying a slow death that has caused thousands of pastors to exit the ministry of the local church.

Deep spiritual change. This is the final, and best, option. Personal change precedes organizational change. You cannot share what you do not have. As pastors we have to walk the talk. Deep spiritual change is what is needed to lead the church today into the future. So then, why do pastors hesitate to embrace deep spiritual change? To answer that question let me tell you a story from the book *Deep Change: Discovering the Leader Within* by Robert E. Quinn ([San Francisco: Jossey-Bass Publishers, 1996], 35).

There was a young family who decided they wanted to go to the zoo. The smallest boy loved playgrounds, especially swings. As soon as they got out of the van, this youngest son made a dash for the swings that were located just outside the zoo. He was having the time of his life.

Before long, the other children were ready to go on into the zoo. The youngest, however, was not ready to leave. His brothers and sisters tried to talk him into leaving but could not. The boy's mother tried to gently talk with her son. She failed to persuade him to let go of the swing and go into the zoo. When the other children began to let everyone know how displeased they were, strangers stopped to watch the drama unfold. The wife looked at her husband and said, "You're this boy's father. Do something!"

The dad remembered that there was a carousel around the corner. He also knew that his son loved to ride on the carousel even more than he liked to swing, and he told his son about it.

Almost every parent can predict what happened next. The boy was not persuaded. The dad's frustration came to a boiling point and "persuasion turned to threat. Finally, the boy was dragged, kicking and squealing, from the swing and continued to protest until the family arrived at the carousel. Suddenly his eyes grew large with excitement. His tears disappeared as he mounted a wooden horse and smiled and waved to his parents."

There are at least three perspectives to this story. First, there is the perspective of the uninvolved passing strangers. The strangers shook their heads, judging the parents who could not succeed without resorting to force. This is the perspective of the uninvolved Monday-morning quarterback. It is easy to judge others when we are not involved.

The second perspective is that of "the two loving but frustrated parents who were struggling to make an intervention in a real situation. The perspective of the responsible actor, trying to make a change in the world," is a challenge for all of us. In theory it looks good, but making change a reality is often filled with frustration and failure.

The third perspective is that of "the self-centered little boy holding tightly to the swing." This little boy is selfish, immature, and afraid of what looks like an uncertain future. I believe the perspective of this little boy is exactly the place where most church leaders find themselves today. It certainly has been true of me. It is painful to think of oneself as the little boy. One of the last things we want to consider is our own selfishness, immaturity, and fear of change. However, most of us are like the little boy who refuses to leave the swing. The more we hear about needed change, the more tightly we grip the swing. What is needed is deep spiritual change in order to confront selfishness, immaturity, and fear. We are to be leaders that walk by faith and not by sight.

When a leader seeks deep spiritual change in his or her own life, there is always God's invitation to walk by faith, not by sight. Jesus said in Matthew 6:33:

> *But strive first for the kingdom of God and his righteousness, and all these things will be given to you as well.* (NRSV)

I am discovering that my relationship with God is similar to other relationships that I value. Any relationship that grows takes time. The relationship with my wife could never grow if we just spoke once in a while. Eileen and I have to make a conscious effort every day to be together so that our relationship can grow. One's relationship with God demands the same if you expect to grow into being a spiritual leader in your church. God has much to teach you and me as this relationship grows and deepens. I know this is something that we pastors often say; unfortunately, we rarely make the relationship with God the number one priority in our lives.

A DAILY TIME FOR GROWING THE RELATIONSHIP WITH GOD

I have found that I must get up each day an hour before my day actually begins. I set my alarm clock an hour earlier than I need to rise each day. I am a fairly weak person; and in the beginning I found that I would often promise myself that if I didn't get up when the alarm sounded, I would then spend my time with God later in the day. My rationalizing went something like this: "I will just sleep another five minutes and then get up." The five minutes usually became an hour. "Well, I will spend my time with God right after I read the morning paper and have breakfast. I don't really have time after breakfast, so I will spend my time with God right after I shower, shave, and get dressed for the day." By then the day had already crowded in on my life. "I have so many tasks to get busy with (messages, letters, appointments, calls, etc.) I will spend my time with God later in the day." You can guess the results. I would never get around to my time with God and usually felt guilty, resolving to do better the next day. The problem was the next day didn't really get better. I knew I had to build in some time of accountability for ensuring my time with God.

Ultimately, I had to remember the principle: *You can't share what you do not have.* Since I am a firstborn child and tend to be very responsible when I tell other people I will do something, I knew the secret for me would be to promise other people that I would pray for them. I decided to write thirty families two weeks before I would pray for them and tell them that on a particular day I would be praying for them. I asked each family to call in prayer requests that I would honor. I also asked each family to pray for me and for our church on a particular day. This meant that during a particular week, I would pray for five families each day. I would do this six days a week. I would pray for thirty families each week and invite each family to pray for our church and me on the day I prayed for them. I find that making a commitment to these five families each day of the week is just the motivation I need to get out of bed an hour earlier each day.

When the alarm goes off I go into the kitchen and start the coffeemaker. In a few minutes I am in my place (a comfortable chair) and ready to begin growing my relationship with God, coffee cup in hand. I like to begin by reading scripture and some devotional material, like Oswald Chambers's *My Utmost for His Highest,* a personal favorite. Then I spend time reading scripture.

Then I begin a routine of prayer conversation that has been used for many years by Christians. It is balanced and easy to use. Remember the word *ACTS*. It is an acronym whose four letters stand for *adoration, confession, thanksgiving,* and *supplication.*

My prayer time begins with *adoration*. This time reminds me who I am addressing and into whose presence I have just entered. I will begin by praising God and often do that with song or music. Frequently, I try to think of every attribute I can. I want God to know I am moving now into God's presence to worship and grow my relationship with God. Reading Psalms 8, 23, 100, or 121 helps me get into focus for this time with God.

During *confession* I try to name the things in my life that have separated me from God in the last twenty-four hours. Have I been arrogant or hurtful to any person? Have I been lazy and not done some of the things I know I should have done? Have I failed to follow Jesus in a focused way throughout the last twenty-four hours? Have I exaggerated to make something sound better than it is? Have I been self-centered, insensitive, or uncaring to anyone, especially to my family? As you might guess, I always have much to confess and lay before God. Confession yields cleansing and the knowledge that God has a forgiving nature. Confession leaves me free to pray that the Holy Spirit will help me give up that sin forever.

Give thanks in all circumstances; for this is the will of God in Christ Jesus for you.
(1 Thessalonians 5:18 NRSV)

The *T* stands for *thanksgiving*. I want to thank God for all the good in my life. I want to thank God for answered prayers. I spend time thanking God for the direction of the Holy Spirit in my life. I want to thank God for my wonderful wife and children. Early in the morning my mind is flooded with feelings of thanksgiving for all that God has allowed in my life. Oddly, I am even thankful for the suffering that has come in my life. I have found that even the hard times and suffering times have been opportunities for God to grow me more into a disciple of Jesus.

In everything by prayer and supplication with thanksgiving let your requests be made known to God.
(Philippians 4:6 NRSV)

Finally, the *S* stands for *supplication.* This is a time to present to God all my requests. Nothing is too big for God to handle or too small for God to care about. God will hear all my requests.

I begin by asking God to "help me be part of what God is blessing." I want to seek first the kingdom of God in all of my life. Then I ask God to "send to Christ Church people that nobody else wants." That is a dangerous prayer to pray because I know that God answers that prayer. All you have to do is look around the church I serve at all the new people who have come to faith. They are a really strange looking group of people. They are nothing like who I would have chosen to be a part of Christ Church.

I now move into different categories. I pray for the ministry of the church. This includes praying, by name, for all the people who work at Christ Church. I then pray for the various ministries. I pray for the funds needed to operate the church another week. I always try to pray with deep gratitude for what God has given through God's people this past Sunday and for guidance that our church will be good stewards of whatever we receive.

I pray that through our ministries God will draw people to Jesus by confronting them with the living Word and saving them from emptiness, brokenness, alienation, and hell. This time of prayer has helped God grow a stronger compassion in me for people who live in darkness.

The next category is for people I have been led to lift up in prayer. This includes denominational leaders, other pastors not on our staff, laypeople with special needs, and our prayer lists generated by the congregation each week.

The category of family is where I pray for my wife, Eileen, and our children. I include all family members in this time of prayer. I also pray for the persons each of my children will marry, even if I do not know that person's name at this time. I ask God for help with decisions that will affect the family.

The last category is where I pray for my needs. I pray that God will shape me more into the character of Jesus with each passing day. I ask God to lead me to people this day who live in darkness and help me to be sensitive to their needs. I ask God to give me patience and lots of love for those people who are in the church, but who nonetheless can be mean and ugly at times because our church is seeking to reach lost people. "Keep me reminded that these people, too, need Jesus," I pray.

Sometimes I write my prayers on the computer. This is especially helpful when I find my mind wandering in the early morning hours. Typing my prayers on the computer keeps my mind focused on the task and also helps me keep awake early in the morning.

Without taking the time to grow your relationship with God, you will find yourself running on "empty" and leading out of your own strengths and talents. You might be a wonderful leader, but in the end you will be empty and broken. Again, *"You can't share what you do not have."*

THE SABBATH DAY FOR STAFF

I have found this morning time to grow my relationship with God so important that I began to think that each staff person needs to know how important spiritual life is in addition to the weekly tasks they do at the church. In order to value each staff person's spiritual life, I suggested to our personnel committee that each staff person be given a

"Sabbath Day" each month in order to grow his or her relationship with God. They agreed, and today we grant one day a month for each staff person to have a day to grow their relationship with God.

On their Sabbath Day, I invite the staff to spend the day with God. I ask them not to use the day to do chores like cleaning the house, shopping, and so forth. I ask them to spend the day with God and to be intentional in growing to be more like Jesus in all of life. I encourage each person to get adequate rest. Sometimes the biggest need one has in the life of the spirit is to get rested. So a person may "sleep in" if he or she chooses. I ask each person to find a place to be alone with God. It might be down by the beach, in their home or apartment, in one of our parks, or any place where one can stop and focus on "walking with God." If asked, I provide devotional suggestions. The Bible is to be the key resource on this day. Some devotional material even provides a guided structure for a day retreat.

Some of our staff are so task driven that to ask them to spend a whole day with God is more than they can do. With these persons, I ask them to spend at least the morning with God; and if that is all the "quiet time" they can handle right now, spend the afternoon doing something in the name of Jesus. I suggest that a person can go to tutor in the public schools in the name of Jesus. A person can go with our feeding ministry and feed homeless people in the name of Jesus. A person can visit homebound older people in the name of Jesus. I want each of our staff to be intentional on this Sabbath Day.

Each Wednesday morning at 11:30 A.M. we have worship with the staff. During that time of worship there is accountability for those persons on the staff who have taken a Sabbath Day the week before. I ask each person to share with the staff exactly what they did with their Sabbath Day and what devotional material they used.

Sabbath Days have helped our entire staff grow to be more Christlike in all that we do as a staff. Sabbath Days have even made nonwork time better for our staff. I want every staff person to know that I value each person's relationship with God. I want us all to be growing in the ways of Jesus.

Principle 11

Growing your relationship with God takes time.

After all, you cannot share what you do not have. It is true of all of us. Each of us must spend the time necessary to grow our relationship with God so our life can reflect Jesus to a broken world.

Being a spiritual leader is learning to trust God and depending on the God who is still actively redeeming a lost world through God's Son, Jesus. Because I believe this so deeply, the most important time on Sundays is the time spent before the worship services begin.

I invite the other pastors and any laypersons who want to join us to meet at 6:30 A.M. on Sundays. We huddle for a few minutes, talk about the day, and have a cup of coffee. We then get to the most important activity on Sunday mornings: we pray. We all go to each of the two places where worship is held on Sundays to pray over every row of chairs in the gym and over each pew in the sanctuary. We pray for the choirs and musicians. We pray for the ushers and greeters.

When I first started this practice, I was alone. When other people heard about this time of prayer, they offered to join me. Initially, I prayed for God to send people to sit in the chairs and pews. I told God we were desperate for people and asked God to send people to fill the chairs and pews. My prayers for each row of chairs and each pew are much different now. Each Sunday now I pray prayers of gratitude for the people God is preparing to send who will sit right on this row. I ask God to help me and all the people of our church participate in doing whatever it is that God would have for the people in this particular row this morning. I ask God to prevent me or any other person from hindering in any way whatever it is that God wants for these people this morning. Words are really inadequate to express how important this beginning time of prayer is for me and the others who join me each week.

This time of prayer can take forty-five minutes to an hour. When we have all finished, it is usually time for us to go to the chapel. There we are joined by more laypeople and the rest of the staff who work on Sunday mornings. We join in fifteen minutes of silent prayer for the day in this holy place. Following this time of prayer the pastors who are preaching are invited to come forward and kneel. All the people in the chapel come forward and lay hands on the pastors as an appointed person offers a prayer for the day and for God to use the pastors who will be bringing the morning messages.

Following this time of prayer one of the pastors leads us in a message and the Sacrament of the Lord's Supper. It is a meaningful time for me each week to be served Holy Communion before beginning this day of worship.

Now we are ready for Sunday morning and all the activity that it brings! A spiritual leader must set the example of the path the people will be invited to follow. Prayer becomes the way God is teaching me to be able to "Walk the Talk." I am being made into a new being.

So if anyone is in Christ, there is a new creation: everything old has passed away; see, everything has become new! (2 Corinthians 5:17 NRSV)

As spiritual leaders, pastors are called to lead their "flock" in the ways of God. I believe that my life must be completely open. I can have no hidden places where there is no accountability for my actions. I have to empower staff and laity to hold me accountable for the way I lead. I know that even though I think of myself as a good person, without accountability and correction, my goodness, like anyone's, can become demonic. It is very important that people feel my encouragement for them to offer a correction.

Roland Sayre is an older member of Christ Church. He has helped the church in many different ways over the years. Sometimes I think every church has a Roland Sayre. If you think about your church, you can probably think of a retired person who comes by every few days to fix things that have broken or to help with a program or ministry. Roland is that kind of helpful person.

The church had asked Roland to be the liaison to the Children's Home that our church supports. We take a special offering every month that has a fifth Sunday and that offering goes to support the Children's Home. The church had just completed a large new addition to our campus. It is our biggest building and has large glass doors at five different points of entrance into the building. Roland asked me one day if he could put posters up on the new glass doors to advertise the Children's Home Sunday. I knew the answer immediately. I said, "No, Roland, these are not bulletin boards, they are large glass entrance doors. I don't want to get this started in the church on our new building. But I will help you out. We have a number of easels, and you can put the posters on them. We can put them in the middle of the sidewalks. More people will see them in the middle of the sidewalks than on the doors anyway." Roland nodded his head and left.

I came over to the church on Saturday morning, and there on all the new glass doors were posters advertising the Children's Home Sunday. This was in direct violation of what I had told Roland. So I took the posters down; and then, because I don't believe in doing things anonymously, I called Roland and told him I had taken them down! I also explained that I would be at church early on Sunday morning, and I would help him get the easels out and put up in the middle of the sidewalks. On Sunday I helped Roland get the easels up. I thought that was the end of that. I had been kind to Roland but firm about the new glass doors of our new building.

About five months later, Darlene Sacks, another layperson, came to me and said, "Dick, we are getting ready for the fall budget campaign. We have these posters, and I want to know if I can put them up on the doors of our new building?" I said, "No, Darlene, I went through this with Roland. The doors are not bulletin boards. We are not going to 'junk up' the doors of our new building. We are not going to get this kind of thing started. If you do it, then everyone else will want to do the same. We have easels, and you can put the posters on the easels in the middle of the sidewalks." Darlene looked at me and said, "Will you pray about this?"

I said, "Yes." I thought to myself that this was a stupid thing to have to bring to God in prayer. I was doing what was best, and I was also offering another way for the person to get the posters out. But since I try to do what I say I will do, I prayed about this matter the next morning.

My prayer went something like this: "Dear God, I don't want to take up a lot of your time with this. I have already dealt with Roland about the same issue. I know you don't want our new glass doors to become bulletin boards, and I have told Roland and Darlene we can use easels; so I won't take up much of your time getting your agreement with me on this. The only reason I am bringing this up is because I told Darlene I would pray about this."

It was as if I heard the voice of God respond, "Say what?" So I started all over with the request, "Dear God, I don't want to take up a lot of your time with this. I have already dealt with Roland about the same issue. I know you don't want our new glass doors to become bulletin boards, and I have told Roland and Darlene we can use easels; so I won't take up much of your time getting your agreement with me on this, etc."

Then it was as if I heard God say to me, "Dick, is this the most important thing you have to bring before me? Are there no people who are suffering in your community? Are there no people who live in darkness not knowing my Son? And you want to know about posters on the glass doors?"

Then I knew. I had a word from God. I knew that the glass doors were not important. I called Darlene and said, "Darlene, I have done as you asked. God told me that the doors were not important. You can put the posters up anywhere you want on the doors. I was wrong."

On Saturday morning I knew that Roland would be there on Sunday and would see the budget campaign posters on the new glass doors. I called Roland on that Saturday morning. I said, "Roland, Darlene wanted to put posters on the new glass doors, and I told her the same thing I told you. Then she asked me to pray about it. I have done that, and God told me I was wrong. I ask for your forgiveness. You can put posters up on the glass doors anytime you want."

Roland responded, "Dick, is that you?" (I don't think Roland thought he was talking to the same pastor he had spoken with a few months earlier.)

I said, "Yes, it's me." Roland said, "Okay, I forgive you." And just as quickly as he said those words he hung up the phone.

The point of this is that the spiritual leader of a congregation has to be accountable for living as Jesus would live, as if Jesus were living inside my body. For me that means always having people challenge me to live in such a way that others can see Jesus in me. I have to be open to correction when I make errors or have priorities that are not Kingdom priorities. *I have to say that I am in the greatest learning curve of my life!* God is teaching me more each day as I grow my relationship with God. Often in that hour or more of quiet time each day, the Lord will give me special guidance and direction.

I want to say I seldom like it when a person comes with

a word of correction. After all, I am a pastor who is trying to do a good and faithful work. As much as I dislike correction and accountability, I must encourage and empower the church to help me grow into the likeness of Jesus. Without their loving help, I am left to rationalize my behavior even when it might be far outside God's will for me.

One day a man who lives in the apartment building across the street parked his old gray van on the grass directly outside the window of my office. It is an ugly van with a white stripe down the side. Our church has let the people who live in that apartment building park on property that the church bought and landscaped. That parking area is just east of my office window and out of my view from my desk. I understand parking is hard to find for those who live in that building. I felt we had accommodated the apartment people enough. The longer the van was parked outside my office window, the more upset I became because as time wore on, it began to kill the grass. One day I saw the van's owner getting in it. I ran outside and explained that his van was killing the grass. I told him that I was aware of the parking problems and that he could park on the church property a block away. He said, "Okay, I would be glad to do that."

But the very next day there was that old ugly gray van with the white stripe down the side parked just outside my window. I saw that ugly van every time I looked up from my desk! I grew more and more irritated. I had done the Christian thing and been kind in offering the man another option. So I began to pray about the unfairness of this man parking his van there and killing our grass.

One morning while praying, it was as if God said to me: "Dick, I am going to leave that van there until you love that man more than you love the grass." I began to pray for that man. This went on for several months. As it did, I learned that if you pray for someone who irritates you, eventually you will begin to love that person. Finally the day came that I looked at the van parked outside my window and felt only love for the man who parked there. The next day the van was gone! It has been parked there only a few times since. Each time, I realize that God has replaced my love of grass with the ability to love that man.

I know that God was teaching me that people are more important than things. I thought I had known that for a long time. What happened was a situation where Kingdom priorities were not really focused in my life. Here was another lesson I had to learn if I was going to be a spiritual leader.

I have deliberately empowered staff and laity to hold me accountable. Everyone in our church is encouraged to give me correction when I wander from Kingdom priorities. Recently a staff person in the office said to me, "You were really good this morning. But this afternoon you blew it. I was disappointed in you the way you handled that situation." She was right, and I asked for forgiveness from God and from her for the "righteous" way in which I had acted. I am making progress, but for a person like me it comes slowly. I am discovering that as I empower people to hold me accountable, I am able to grow more in the ways of obedience as a disciple of Jesus.

I am learning to listen to people who have a "walk with God." When I am held accountable "in love," I have learned to trust that the person who speaks the hard words of correction does so for my benefit and for the benefit of our church. I really think most pastors would be surprised to realize how many laypersons really want us to be spiritual leaders in the best sense of that term.

In this time of great growth there have been two serendipities. First, I began to have clear priorities for my life and for our church. This is a process that requires time and attention to biblical principles. With the help of Scripture and a lot of people, biblical principles are becoming the priorities for me and for our church.

Second, I am not afraid. All through the Bible we hear

the words, "Do not be afraid." The more I walk with God, the less fear I have. I cannot emphasize enough the joy that comes from not being afraid or anxious like I used to be. I know I walk with a God whom I can trust. As the psalmist says:

> *The LORD is my shepherd, I shall not be in want.*
> *He makes me lie down in green pastures,*
> *he leads me beside quiet waters,*
> *he restores my soul.*
> *He guides me in paths of righteousness*
> *for his name's sake.*
> *Even though I walk*
> *through the valley of the shadow of death,*
> *I will fear no evil,*
> *for you are with me;*
> *your rod and your staff,*
> *they comfort me.*   (Psalm 23:1-4 NIV)

UNDERSTAND THE COST

If you come to visit Christ Church, you will see a church where people love God and love others. The buildings are nicely kept. The organization runs pretty smoothly. Most weeks everything looks great, especially if you come from a church that is plateaued or dying. All of the good that you see at Christ Church happens, but not without a cost. Jesus said we are to understand the cost. There is a cost involved in being a spiritual leader. You will remember that Jesus said:

> *Whoever does not carry the cross and follow me cannot be my disciple. For which of you, intending to build a tower, does not first sit down and estimate the cost, to see whether he has enough to complete it? Otherwise,*

93

> *when he has laid a foundation and is not able to finish,*
> *all who see it will begin to ridicule him, saying, "This*
> *fellow began to build and was not able to finish."*
> *(Luke 14:27-30 NRSV)*

I do not dwell on the negatives very much. In thinking of Christ Church I had to go back and remember the "costs" for being the spiritual leader. There are many, but I will mention only a few of them. It is very important that you understand the costs if you seek to be a spiritual leader.

First, I remember the loneliness and pain of being a spiritual leader. I know well the pain of having people I care about and love leave the church because I sought to be faithful to biblical principles of where the church needed to change. These wonderful people had grown comfortable in a church that was safe, predictable, and dying. The spiritual renewal and conversion I had experienced in South Africa was met with distance and anger by some of the people I loved the most. Their leaving the church was and is very painful to me.

I remember the pain of having a very focused death threat left for me on my voice mail at the church. Someone disliked me very much! It was an interesting experience. It was at the point in my life that I realized that no human being could take my life because I had already given it to God. I tried to be careful in the next few months, but I was not afraid. God is good!

I also remember the pain of having a person I loved very much begin to hate me for my leadership. Let's say this person's name is "Ted." Ted was a leader in the church. To this day I do not know exactly what provoked such hatred in Ted. Rather than leave, he continued to stay in the church and worked to undermine my leadership. One Sunday, one of our pastors announced that another pastor (from Christ Church) and I had been elected to represent our denomination at its national meeting. The congregation broke into applause. But Ted's demeanor at the time made it clear to all who could see him (and a lot of folks could see him) that he disapproved strongly. I truly felt bad for him. I know that Jesus told us to love our enemies.

But I tell you who hear me: Love your enemies, do good to those who hate you, bless those who curse you, pray for those who mistreat you. (Luke 6:27-28 NIV)

I began to pray for Ted every day. I prayed that God would bless his life and fill his life with only good things and lots of love. I prayed that God would heal any hurt in his life and surround him always with love. If you pray a prayer like that every day, you will find in a year or two you will only feel love for that person. God will change the hurt and anger of someone hating you to genuine love for that person. This is exactly what happened to me. I feel only love for Ted. I am sad when he speaks against me with such hatred, but I do not feel hatred in return.

I also went to this brother to ask for his forgiveness for anything I had ever said or done to hurt him or his family. I did this on at least six different occasions, but he was still unwilling to forgive me and relinquish his hatred. At one point a group of leaders of our church met with Ted to ask him to desist from his hatred of me and my leadership. Rather than receiving their counsel, Ted only seemed to hate me more.

One morning I was praying for Ted, and God seemed to tell me to ask Ted to go to lunch. I thought to myself, "Oh no, Ted will only spew his hatred at me one more time." Still I knew that I must invite him to lunch. I did so, and sure enough, at lunch he proceeded to tell me all the reasons he hated me. Once again I asked for his forgiveness for anything I had done or said that had hurt him or his family. I shared that I wanted us to be friends again. That did not help. The next morning I was praying for Ted, and God again seemed to say, "Dick, that was good that you took Ted to lunch. Now I want you to do that once each month for a year." I can tell you I thought that leading from God was a mistake. But I invited Ted faithfully once each month for a year. As the months passed, Ted began to tell more about his family and childhood. I felt his heart begin to soften toward me. Then one day he said, "Dick, I don't want to hate you anymore." I told him that together we could make a great team at our church if he would only forgive me. I honestly did not know and still do not know exactly why Ted hates me so. But I am clear that when there is a broken relationship, assigning blame is unimportant. The focus is always on how to restore the relationship. That is why I continued to ask Ted's forgiveness for anything I had done or said that had hurt him or his family.

On that day, I thought God had performed the miracle for which I had been praying. Because of his behavior, the lay leadership in the church were firm that Ted was not to have a leadership position for at least six months to ensure that God had done a redeeming work in his heart. Ted was better for a couple of months. Then one day he demanded a meeting with all the ministry staff. In that meeting he was filled again with hatred for things that had happened eleven years earlier. There were even some items that happened before I came to Christ Church that Ted felt were my fault as well. As the meeting ended, I was filled with sadness. I had been so hopeful that God had done a miracle in Ted's heart. God did do a miracle. It was not the miracle that I wanted. Ted still hates me. The miracle that God did was in me. God gave me only love for Ted. Recently, after six years of Ted's focused hatred, he started attending another church. I seldom see Ted these days. I still pray for him every day. My heart continues to be filled with love for him and his family. If you pray God's blessings for your enemy every day, then within a year or two God's gift of grace to you will be to take away your hurt and anger and to enable you to feel love for that person. God's ways are truly not our ways. Spiritual leaders will have to bear crosses if they are becoming fully devoted followers of Jesus.

Another area of pain has come from my brothers and sisters in the ministry. It has been very painful to find that some people I considered to be good friends have been so negative about me in other clergy circles. It is painful to have a clergy friend demean what God is doing in the lives of people at Christ Church. I have to pray for God's love to be in the hearts of these friends. A part of the cost has been long periods of time when the church did not receive the financial resources that would enable us to pay our denominational obligations. In order to deal with the shortage of funds in a biblical way, I instructed our business administrator to send to the denomination 12 percent of whatever we received in the weekend offerings. This check was mailed into the denomination each week on Tuesday morning. If we did not have enough funds to meet our denominational obligations, then we were going to demonstrate the same kind of financial faithfulness that we were asking our people to demonstrate in their tithe to the church. For many years even this faithful giving did not allow us to pay out our denominational obligations. Only in the last three years have we paid out 100 percent. It is painful when you are faithful and all that you need does not come when you think you need it.

Because we struggled so many years financially, the cost to me was not receiving a salary raise for seven of the thirteen years I have been at Christ Church. I make a very good salary, so I don't want you to think that I suffered. But when the other clergy in your denomination are getting raises, it is painful not to be able to receive one. In recent years I have declined raises offered to me by the church. As I prayed about this, I simply felt that I made enough money as a pastor and that I did not need to make any more.

Christ Church has been through some tough times. In 1991, the two-story educational building burned on the last Sunday available to raise the funds for our new $3.6

million Life Enrichment Center. We would have to move the church offices to an office building and then delay the Life Enrichment Center a year while the educational building was being rebuilt. Then, finally on the Sunday we were to break ground on the Life Enrichment Center, Hurricane Andrew roared through South Florida pushing back the beginning of the building for another three months.

My own most painful moments came in October of 1993. The Life Enrichment Center was completed. During August and September our income was less than our expenses. I wanted to meet with the leaders of the church for a quick meeting after church just to let them know of the situation so that, if this trend continued, some folks could be working on it and not be surprised. I have always tried to make sure that I don't have stressful meetings when I am tired. I thought that right after church would be a good time to have a ten-minute meeting even though I was tired. I was surprised to find that this "ten minute" meeting went on for over an hour. The leaders of the church began to question every little decision that was being made. I tried to be patient with them for more than an hour. It was clear that what really was being questioned was my leadership. I had been at Christ Church for seven years at this point. Coupled with my exhaustion and irritated with this new distrust of leadership, I "drew a line in the sand." I told them they were proud that the church fed seventy homeless people Thursday evenings. I went on say that when God sees what we are doing, God is insulted. A large church like ours is only feeding seventy people? A church like ours should be feeding hundreds of people. I indicated that as a church, we were not even approaching what God had in mind for us. I then told them they would have to decide if they wanted to follow my leadership. Maybe they should get themselves another pastor. (The line was drawn.) I concluded by saying I did not know what *they* would do about *their* financial problems. I left and slammed the door on my way out.

The staff sat there stunned at what they had just witnessed. I was the leader who had just said, "This is the way north. If you want another direction for north, then get yourself another leader!" I was devastated. Seven years of hard work was now gone. I went home weeping and told Eileen that we were moving as soon as possible. I was a terrible failure at this church. The bishop would be called and I would leave right away. At 2:00 P.M. Sunday afternoon I cried and cried until I drifted into a light sleep. Later that afternoon concerned people from the church began coming to the house. I refused to see anyone. I was broken and was a failure after seven years of hard work. I did have dinner with good friends that evening and tried to mask the deep pain in my soul. The next morning I went to a clergy "School of Ministry," which was to last four days. I shared with two close clergy friends my complete sense of failure and the deep woundedness failure brings to the human spirit. In many ways it was a very lonely week, even though I was among hundreds of pastors.

When I returned to Fort Lauderdale, laypeople came to me and asked who it was that would have questioned my leadership. These laity were going to go and confront the leaders who had met with me on that Sunday after church. I told them that I was perfectly able to take care of myself. I did not need to be rescued! I did not need for them to go and confront anybody! They would have to decide if they wanted to follow my leadership in discerning what God's will was for our church. Again I was saying gently but firmly, "Decide who you want to be the leader to help you discern God's will for this church."

Generally, in the United States of America we raise leaders up to tear them down. I find it true in the secular world and also true in the church. I believe what happened on that Sunday in 1993 was a moment of truth for me and our church. I can only say that God was active in what would happen next. I am not sure how it happened, but from that point on the leadership of the church granted me the authority to be the spiritual leader of our church. I believe that God was at work in the lives of the people. People need spiritual leadership. Through the grace of God, I was given the authority to be the spiritual leader of our church. Like all of my journey at Christ Church, it is a gift from God. Since that time my leadership has not been seriously questioned. We are discerning God's will, and this is "the way North." From this deep sense of failure and brokenness has come the ability to grow toward being the spiritual leader of this congregation. I never dreamed such a possibility existed. I was sure brokenness and failure were to be the mark of my ministry at this church. God had a different idea. In a profound way I was allowed to be wounded and broken that day so that God could perform a miracle of resurrection. I understand now that it was all part of the cost of being a spiritual leader. Never, never, underestimate God's power and ability to bring good out of suffering.

And we know that in all things God works for the good of those who love him, who have been called according to his purpose.   (Romans 8:28 NIV)

The first Sunday in October 1993 was a watershed moment in the life of this church. That day I understood clearly the cross, and I felt broken by it. God had other things in mind than my failure and brokenness. I know you and I can trust the goodness of God in all things.

Another cost is having to wait on God's timing for growth, staff, and ministries. Often I feel like I know what God is leading us to do, but the necessary pieces are not there to make it happen. I am learning to trust God in more and more of life in the church and life outside of the church. God's timetable is often so much slower than I would like.

Our youth pastor left one May to go to seminary. God knows how important a youth pastor is to our church. I thought that if I prayed, God would send us the right youth pastor before the youth ministry declined. I was wrong. I prayed every day for months. We interviewed 122 persons. A few we invited to come, and for various reasons each took other positions in other churches. By December the youth group had dwindled down to about thirty young people. Two weeks before we were losing our last part-time helper, Peter's name turned up by way of the Internet, and he applied for the position. Peter has turned out to be God's answer to the many months of prayer. He began the position in January, and I know that we are completely within God's will with his leadership. In two weeks the youth group was back to more than one hundred young people. What I am learning is that part of the cost is learning to wait for God's timing. Everything works best when God is in charge. But the cost is found in the waiting. Jesus said:

"And whoever does not take up the cross and follow me is not worthy of me." (Matthew 10:38 NRSV)

For spiritual leaders, the cross is not something laid upon us by God. It is something we must pick up. As with everything else in our walk with God, it begins with a decision. As a spiritual leader, as soon as we decide to fulfill the specific purpose God has for us, we pick up our cross. It is not necessary that we should know what God's purpose is. It is necessary only that we decide to fulfill it.

To pick up my cross, I must learn to lay down my right to myself. Gradually, it dawns upon a spiritual leader that good work does not produce fruit. Dying to self and doing God's will produces fruit.

As spiritual leaders, we can't use Jesus as a means to a better lifestyle. We can't expect God's power to flow through us to acquire a better position or to have financial gain. Spiritual leaders are simply available to be used by God for a particular purpose with a particular people.

When you begin to understand how God will use you, the first reaction a person usually feels is disbelief. It is not that a person does not believe in a godly purpose, rather one just doesn't believe he or she is the one who can fulfill it. Spiritual leaders are most aware of their own weaknesses, and it is beyond comprehension that they could accomplish anything worthwhile for God.

This is not unusual, because we have forgotten or never known that God always asks us to do what is impossible. It is only possible if we depend on God for a miracle. God always wants a spiritual leader to be the kind of person that will depend on God.

God never tells what God's ultimate purpose is for the life of the spiritual leader. If one had the answer to that question, one would rush out and immediately get to work on it. The spiritual leader realizes if God told him or her God's goal for the leader, the leader would no longer keep eyes focused upon God. One would become consumed by one's own efforts to accomplish the goal.

This is frustrating. (If you doubt this, just listen to your brothers and sisters in the ministry constantly asking God to tell them God's will for their lives.) So we busy ourselves with worthwhile projects, hoping to get a "nod" of approval from God.

Sooner or later, it dawns on us that God is not project-oriented. God is not interested in our spurts of "good work" activity. God's purpose takes shape in direct proportion to the consistency of one's commitment. As I focus on God, waiting for God's direction at each step, God unfolds revelation moment by moment. I can look back and see how God has directed my steps to bring me to where I am, but I can look forward only as far as God can trust me.

I am learning that when I follow Jesus, I am on the way to fulfilling God's purpose in my life. I am aware that my focus shifts away from my own physical, emotional, and spiritual problems. This is because God frees me from my limited self, and I can begin to see life from God's perspective. The sad state of the world seems to be overwhelming. I am realizing that somehow, in some way known only to God, I have a part in God's redemptive process.

God's Word begins to sink in:

For by him all things were created: things in heaven and on earth, visible and invisible, whether thrones or powers or rulers or authorities; all things were created by him and for him.　　　　　　(Colossians 1:16 NIV)

It occurs to me that the Jesus I received at conversion exists within me to fulfill God's purpose. I cannot accomplish this on my own, but Jesus in me has no problem accomplishing it, because he does only what he sees the Father do. He has set the standard for obedience. Therefore, when I give Jesus dominion, he accomplishes the will of the Father. This makes me his disciples, and the Father is glorified, because I can bear much fruit (John 15:8).

I am learning as this takes place, there may be no conscious effort on my part of what is happening. It is simply the inevitable result of my abiding relationship with Jesus. This makes me a useful vessel as a spiritual leader of God's people.

God lets me see God's divine principle that all things function through Jesus (Romans 11:36). Anything not done through Jesus is temporal and passes away. Jesus is the reason for the life of the spiritual leader. He overcomes everything natural within us, so the will of God is fulfilled in our lives.

FOR REFLECTION

1. Would you say that you are a spiritual leader? Why? Why not?

2. What would have to change in your life for you to become a spiritual leader?

3. Are there people you could ask to hold you accountable and to encourage you (all done in love)?

4. Are there people in your church who dislike you that you could begin to pray for daily?

5. What in this chapter spoke to you? Why?

CONCLUSION

Sometimes I think people have been taught to love their religion or their denomination more than God. When that happens, their religion or denomination becomes the focus of their dedication, and even the object of their worship. Contrast this with the apostles who had no denomination on which to focus, no full-blown systematic theology to study, nor even a New Testament from which to preach. All they had was Jesus, and it was him they preached.

In fact they preached that a personal relationship was possible with God through Jesus. But many of us pastors often get caught up in trying to please our people rather than being in relationship with God and leading those among whom we minister to be in that same relation. Jesus said:

> If you love me, you will obey what I command.
> (John 14:15 NIV)

Notice that love comes before obedience. Do we not so often look for ways to obey him so we can come into right relationship and demonstrate our love for him? But Jesus says if we come into relationship with him we receive his love. This enables us to love him, and the natural outcome will be to obey him. Love comes before obedience. It is not the other way around.

One of the greatest quests for all serious Christians is to discover the will of God for their lives. But we never discover his will as long as our focus is on the "discovery" rather than upon him. We know that it is his will for us to produce fruit that glorifies the Father and proves we are his disciples (John 15:8). How can we do this if we do not know him?

My greatest hope for this book is not that you will find a new model of ministry, a kind of spiritual blueprint, for your church. *Rather my hope is that this book has opened to you the possibility of spiritual leadership that is based on a relationship with God through Jesus.*

I believe there are biblical and spiritual principles that can guide you in this relationship, which are foundational to becoming a spiritual leader. I hope that I have shared some of them in helpful ways for you. These principles can become some starting points in helping you and your church live into a role that God desires.

For some, this book will mean stepping away from traditional ways of understanding the church and how it functions. We have all been called, as disciples, to be fishers of men and women. Unlike other fishermen, we are not instructed (in God's church) to weigh, measure, and record our catches. We are simply to present them to Jesus to do with as he pleases. After all, the church belongs to God. My hope is that all of us who are leaders and pastors in the church will belong to God as well. This is my one desire, and I will pray that it will also be your one desire.

AFTERWORD

by Beverly Payne, Member of Christ Church

Christ Church, 1970, . . . wow! People lined up at the doors to go in to hear a great message, a sanctuary larger than any we'd ever been in, and a full time hostess/cook for all the church dinners! Quite a new experience for a young Midwest family only five years off the farm!

Because of its close proximity to our rented house, Christ Church drew us on our first Sunday in Fort Lauderdale. Having left a small congregation in St. Paul, Minnesota, when we ventured to Florida for a job opportunity, we determined to visit every church in the area before we settled in to a new church home. But Dr. Paul Brown, the retired part-time associate, hooked us with his bold preaching of the Word. Before we knew it, we had walked down front two weeks later to join. Little did we know that he was not the primary "drawing card" to this beautiful church around the corner from the country club.

Yes, Christ Church did have the appearance and feel of a "country club" church once it became more familiar to us as our church home. Cars, clothes, and affluence like we'd never experienced abounded. The ministries were flourishing under the direction of committed staff like Martha Renfro and Tom Hamilton. The choir was glorious under the direction of Geraldine Curphey. And the children's ministries were full of young-family offspring. Women's circles, United Methodist Men, and the youth program were always busy with fundraisers and activities. It was a wonderful church home for fellowship, food (lots of church dinners), and involvement. It wasn't missing anything visible—at least not to those busy about its activities.

But as is oftentimes the case, if something looks too good to be true, it usually is. Traumas began to plague the congregation. The departure of a member of the church staff, under very serious accusations, seemed to open a floodgate of rumors and some truths that began to tear the church apart. With the assignment of the senior minister to another large church because of substantiated serious concerns, Christ Church began to face a long period of trials. Membership rolls were cleared of a few hundred deceased "members" and the congregation began to work on maintaining those who remained. Those were not easy years.

The senior ministers appointed to the church during those years had their hands full trying to heal the wounds of some and please others. Committees formed and met with a vengeance, mainly to assure the congregation that things would not happen unknown to the members. But that didn't squelch the problems—more staff members were dismissed due to personal time spent in inappropriate activities, and the trials continued. Throughout those years there were committed laypersons whose fervent prayers for the ministers and congregation continued. Their hearts were assured of God's presence in the midst of the struggles, but their efforts seemed futile and frustrating with the frequent change of leadership in key ministry areas. The spiritual temperature fluctuated with the degree of challenges facing the faithful. Those whose hope was in a person tended to leave when that person left. Those who were faithful to God's will for Christ Church continued to pray and struggle.

During the past twenty-five years, Christ Church has experienced significant change in the vision, spirituality, and makeup of the congregation. For many, it has been a long process from knowing Jesus Christ is the reason for attending church and being involved to knowing Jesus Christ in a personal relationship. Jesus has moved from the heads to the hearts of most Christ Church members today. It is a personal relationship with Jesus Christ that has led members to hear the call of God for their lives. This has resulted to a great degree from the spiritual leadership of our present senior pastor, Dick Wills.

Life was not so great when Dick Wills came to Christ Church. He came at another time of crisis in the life of the church, and unhappy members appeared to be in the majority. A beloved staff member was dying of an incurable disease and unable to continue in the responsibilities of the position. With his termination of active employment, another overwhelmingly tough issue split a large portion of the membership. Once again, hope had been put in a person, and some left with him.

Reverend Wills had a comforting, assured demeanor when he came to Christ Church and seemed to fare well under the scrutiny and hard questioning of some members. His efforts appeared to be in helping to heal a hurting congregation while trying to maintain the financial stability that had broken down so many times during the years of crises. Because of his work to pull things back together, there were some who thought he surely had too much control. Basically, there was a serious need for someone to be fair but firm, and Dick Wills was in the responsible position. Thankfully, Dick was supported by many who recognized the need for his strong leadership, because that too became a point of contention for some.

When Dick was invited to participate in a conference in South Africa, no one really understood its purpose or the honor it was for him to be invited. In fact, many didn't even know how the church could afford for him to go, in time or dollars. But what was recognized was that Dick came back inspired to hire a minister from South Africa along with his wife, a rottweiler, and a cat named Mozart! As a member of the staff-parish committee at the time, I couldn't imagine what had happened that Christ Church would go to that expense! But as God's will began to unfold, without our clearly recognizing God in the midst, Rowan and Liz Rogers came to Christ Church and helped to begin a transformation of the membership through their testimony and witness to us. And Dick Wills had experienced a similar transformation while in South Africa and sensed the need for it at home in Fort Lauderdale.

With the first training for Wesley Fellowship Group leaders in 1992 under the direction of Rowan Rogers, it became obvious that Dick was taking a backseat to what he felt was God's will and direction. He clearly stepped aside for God to work through Rowan to reach so many church members with a new and deep spiritual calling. And Dick participated in the learning and then the leading! It was a wonderful time of growth for the staff and congregation of Christ Church.

In Wesley Fellowship Groups, we were encouraged to share our lives, hold each other accountable, pray together, study scripture, and commit ourselves to outreach. We were also made aware that to share our experience with others, we would need to "parent" and "grandparent" new groups to fulfill our commitment.

Out of these close-knit groups, individuals began to feel and know that God had a specific plan for their lives. Persons began to experience God's call to lead and do things far beyond their felt capabilities. When presenting this call to Dick Wills, the response was always, "Pray about it." We were asked to pray for specific concerns, requests, and people necessary to fulfill God's call to lead a ministry.

With this commitment to outreach and God's call on persons' lives, we began ministries unlike any in prior years:

- Clothing Connection (receiving, sorting, sizing donated clothing for distribution to agencies and shel-

ters within the community), which now clothes approximately two thousand people each month
• Homeless Feeding twice a week to the beach area and "Tent City" residents, serving up to 750 meals weekly
• Shepherd's Way ministry to help homeless people to independence through housing, employment, food, and child-care support

For those of us in leadership positions in the church, it was apparent that Dick Wills' experience in South Africa had made a profound change in his life and in his leadership style, and now was affecting every person at Christ Church. Every committee person was asked to pray about decisions before final determinations were made. This included times of silent prayer during meetings.

Soon Dick was making us aware that he would be away for a week, praying and fasting, to seek God's will for his messages and for Christ Church. We were asked to keep him in our prayers and also to pray for God's will at Christ Church. All of this committed us to a closer walk with God in our prayer life, which was the beginning of great changes in our leadership styles.

Without really understanding why and how we were changing, many of us were quite overwhelmed when asked to pray about being Lay *Pastors* for our various areas of ministry, including Wesley Fellowship Group leaders. The concept was that we would shepherd others within our groups and committees to deeper spiritual growth by beginning each gathering with prayer and seeking to fulfill God's vision for Christ Church:

• To introduce people to Jesus in positive ways
• To disciple believers through Wesley Fellowship Groups
• To relieve suffering

We were required to set time for personal daily prayer and scripture reading. Another commitment we made was to attend a monthly LIGHT (Leadership in God's Holy Training) gathering for teaching from our senior pastor Dick Wills. This is always a meeting opened with praise singing and a time to share what God is doing in the lives of persons within our ministry areas. An invitation to this learning experience was, and is, extended to anyone who wishes to attend, so that Christ Church is always open to hear and share God's call to ministry in each person's life. Our prayer is always to be a part of what God is blessing, and as a group we both question and affirm each other's sharing as we commit to join in praying for the call.

It was apparent with the first large group of laity who were consecrated as Lay Pastors, that God was at work in the lives of people at Christ Church. With the openness, encouragement, and support of Dick Wills (and the staff, who also experienced change and spiritual growth during this time), laypersons truly began to lead Christ Church. Our Administrative Board was the first to adopt the policy of seeking God's will through prayer and discernment rather than voting, except in *Discipline*-directed issues.

The Leaders' Council (the visionary group) had replaced the Council of Ministries in the early years of Dick Wills' ministry at Christ Church. Now it became the beginning of a more team-oriented leadership style in the church, which has permeated all aspects of ministry groups including the staff. Each Lay Pastor has a staff team member to turn to for advice and counsel, but those needs are minimal with the opportunity to share, report, and request prayer at the monthly LIGHT meetings.

Meetings at Christ Church have taken on a new look over the past few years. Monday nights are reserved for committee meetings that must take place. By limiting meetings to one night a week, the emphasis is on personal involvement in ministry throughout the week. This concept has allowed busy people to commit to outreach ministry on week nights when they otherwise might have been sitting in committee meetings. Decisions are now a matter of specific prayer and listening for God's word to us.

An interesting change that has resulted from prayer-centered response to God's call on the lives of people is that there no longer seems to be a need to recruit volunteers or to persuade people to fill positions. Parishioners come forward with a desire to serve in answer to God's call. And if no one steps out on a particular considered need, it is frequently determined that possibly the time is not right for that ministry or that a step of faith and continued prayer is in order to discern God's will.

The "heart" of Christ Church is now full of compassion for our hurting world and centered on what God would have us do and be. Involvement in ministries reaching out to others has made significant changes in surprising places. New leadership in worship includes a Men's Chorus (resulting from an active Promise Keepers group) under the direction of a former nightclub entertainer (brought to Christ Church by a woman he was interested in dating) who has committed his life to Jesus Christ and is studying for the ministry. Praise music, including electric guitars, drums, tambourines, and other formerly unlikely instruments at Christ Church, draws more and more seekers to three different praise services. The bulletin used in the sanctuary services is complete with words to hymns, prayers, and creeds, making it more inviting to those who are not familiar with church service protocol and hymnals. Scripture is often quoted from easy-to-understand translations to eliminate explanation. And people know when they leave that they've been a part of a vibrant, loving, serving congregation.

Christ Church, 1999, . . . wow! People lined up at the doors to go out as servants with a great message to a hurting world, services in the chapel and gymnasium as well as the sanctuary, and a lay ministry of committed servants preparing and taking food to hundreds of God's homeless people each week! Yes, Christ Church is a changed place and a changed people, and God has allowed me to be a part of this awesome blessing.